AMERICAN PRISONER OF WAR CAMPS
IN COLORADO

KATHY KIRKPATRICK

AMERICA
THROUGH TIME®
ADDING COLOR TO AMERICAN HISTORY

America Through Time is an imprint of Fonthill Media LLC
www.through-time.com
office@through-time.com

Published by Arcadia Publishing by arrangement with Fonthill Media LLC
For all general information, please contact Arcadia Publishing:
Telephone: 843-853-2070
Fax: 843-853-0044
E-mail: sales@arcadiapublishing.com
For customer service and orders:
Toll-Free 1-888-313-2665

www.arcadiapublishing.com

First published 2020

Copyright © Kathy Kirkpatrick 2020

ISBN 978-1-63499-261-9

Typeset in Minion Pro 10pt on 13pt
Printed and bound in England

Contents

List of Illustrations

Introduction

America is a nation of immigrants, so hosting prisoners of war (POWs) from their homelands brought mixed feelings among the civilians and military in the communities where the prisoners were housed and worked. For many farmers who had immigrated to the Midwest, being able to contract for German POW labor not only eased the labor shortage, but it also brought the opportunity to speak their native language, perhaps to learn about family and friends left behind when they immigrated to America. It also often gave them the opportunity to provide additional food for men who worked hard for them and shared their friendship. Although these Americans had sons fighting in the war, they were more aware of the lack of choices these German prisoners had in their own lives than those who had not left an oppressive homeland.

The same situation applied to Italian immigrants and Italian POWs with the additional benefit of a less strained relationship after Italy became a part of the Allied cause in September 1943. The resulting friendships (and some marriages) show the very positive results of their experiences under very difficult circumstances.

In fact, when German-American or Italian-American families were given permission to hire Prisoners of War to work on their farms or canneries, they were being given a measure of approval often missing in their own communities. In 1940, 330, 000 Germans and 694,000 Italians had registered as aliens. Those not living on the coasts were not displaced, but suffered the name-calling and ostracism promoted by the government and media directed at those groups of people during that time to promote the war effort. They could be arrested just for translating English into German for an aged grandparent.

DON'T SPEAK THE ENEMY'S LANGUAGE

The four freedoms are not in their vocabulary!

SPEAK AMERICAN

From "una Storia Segreta" by Lawrence Distasi. The licensing metadata from the picture claims that it is a "work prepared by an officer or employee of the United States Government as part of that person's official duties."

The stories shared in the course of researching this topic include a moving description by a young Girl Scout raising the flag while a truck load of prisoners passes by, with tears in their eyes. Even as a child, she understood that those men deeply loved and missed their children now living in harm's way.

Following the war, some of these farm families corresponded with the former prisoners until their deaths. A treasure trove of about 350 letters and photos from German former prisoners has recently been discovered in a home in Tennessee. They are now housed at the Lipscomb University in Nashville. They met by working on that farm, and kept in touch over the years. However, it was secret. The letters were found in a cereal box in a closet and even the children of this woman didn't know about them.

For many years into the 1970s and 1980s, and as late as 2009, there were reunions and family trips made by former prisoners to their old camps and the farms where they worked. They also visited the graves of their comrades who did not survive to go home at the end of the war.

Of the half-million German immigrants arriving in the United states from 1947-1960, several thousand had spent time here as prisoners of war. The same can be said of Italian immigrants after World War II. They had friends and good experiences here that motivated them to move here themselves.

Even among those Enemy Aliens who were forced to repatriate at the end of World War II in exchange for Americans and for other reasons, the vast majority had agreed to the arrangement because it guaranteed them the ability to return to the U.S. at a later date. They later used that agreement to return home to the United States. That included Germans, Italians, and Japanese.

Prisoners were moved between Service Command Areas in 1943 as the U.S. built more camps and received more prisoners from overseas. Later, the prisoners were moved within a Service Command as necessary to provide seasonal labor on farms and in canneries as well as other work necessary for civilians as well as the military population.

Using a variety of sources in the United States and Italy, the complete story will be told. Sources cited include military records now housed at the National Archives II (in College Park, MD), documents from the Italian Army Archives in Rome (Stato Maggiore Esercito), *L'Ufficio Informazione Vaticano per I prigionieri di guerra istituto da Pio XII* in the Vatican Secret Archives, as well as many books, articles, websites, and photographs.

Also utilized are interviews with former POWs, guards, translators (and their families) and many other sources both published and unpublished. Their experiences will also be compared to those of German POWs and internees held in America during World War I.

Above: Entrance to the Vatican Secret Archives. [*Photo by author*]

Below: German Prisoners of War at Fort Douglas (UT) in 1917 (crews of German ships). [*Courtesy of Utah Historical Society*]

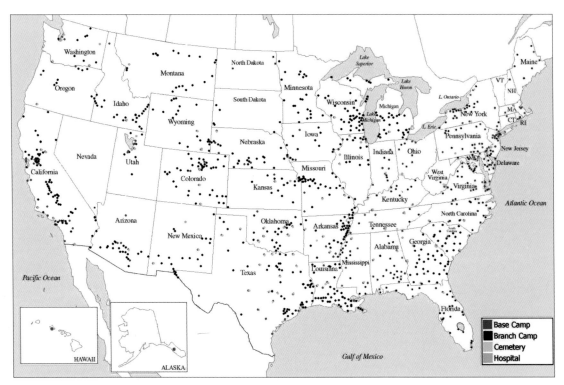

Map of POW Camps and Hospitals Across America. [*Courtesy of John Saffell*]

1

Background

By the time we entered World War II (WWII), almost the whole world was at war. This situation included large numbers of POWs which could no longer be supported by the limited resources of the British and French who captured many of them, primarily in North Africa in 1939.

The U.S. had already prepared plans for camps to house large numbers of enemy aliens, so assisting with prisoners captured by the British was easily incorporated into those general plans. It was determined early that the U.S. would not be imprisoning as many enemy aliens as first planned. The number of resident aliens who matched the original enemy alien profile was much larger than anticipated, so implementing that original plan was not possible.

During World War I (WWI), only 1,346 POWs were held on United States soil. They were the crews of German military ships lying in U.S. ports when the war began. They were held in the same three locations as civilian enemy aliens, plus six additional branch locations for a total of 5,887 prisoners of war. All other prisoners of that war captured by the U.S. were held in France.

Those U.S. locations included the following:

War Prison Barracks #1 - Fort McPherson, East Point, GA - 100 prisoners maximum
War Prison Barracks #2 - Fort Oglethorpe, Catloosa County, GA - 800 prisoners maximum
War Prison Barracks #3 - Fort Douglas, Salt Lake City, UT – 406 POWs and 786 enemy aliens

On March 21, 1918, the POWs were transferred from Fort Douglas to Fort McPherson. On July 19, 1919, 108 conscientious objectors arrived at Fort Douglas from Fort Leavenworth, KS. They were housed in the compound left vacant by the POWs.

Branch camps under the camps in GA:
Camp Devens, Ayer, MA - 100 prisoners maximum
Camp Grant, Rockford, IL - 100 prisoners maximum
Camp Jackson, Columbia, SC - 100 prisoners maximum
Camp Sevier, Greenville, SC - 100 prisoners maximum
Camp Sherman, near Chillicothe, OH - 100 prisoners maximum
Camp Wadsworth, Spartanburg, SC - 100 prisoners maximum

Monument to German POWs from WWI at Fort Douglas, UT. The U.S. did not separate the Enemy Aliens from the POWs, so only two of the twenty-one men on this list were POWs. [*Photo by author*]

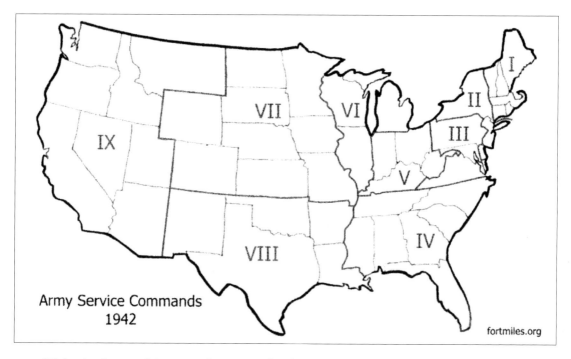

U.S. Service Command Areas map, from National Archives and Records Administration II in College Park, MD, Record Group 389

These camps were run by the Provost Marshal General's Office (PMGO) of the U.S. Army. Initially, there were no distinctions between captured German sailors and enemy aliens rounded up from across the U.S. However, it soon became apparent that the two groups were quite different and efforts were made to put different groups into different camps.

Another camp, called an Internment Camp, was established at Hot Springs, NC, and run by the Immigration and Naturalization Service (INS). It held 2,200 Germans from commercial ships in U.S. ports when war broke out in 1914. They were placed at Hot Springs in May 1917 for the remainder of the war. Burials from this location were removed to Chattanooga National Cemetery after that war.

Preparing for War

The military headquarters and training for the Ninth Service command moved inland from the Presidio of San Francisco, CA to Fort Douglas, UT at the end of 1941 to make it less vulnerable to a Japanese attack.

The US needed:

1. Labor, since most able-bodied young men were expected in military service and efforts to recruit women into the workforce had only limited success. However, "Rosie the Riveter" became iconic and female pilots as well as clerks (military and civilian), nurses, teachers, and many other occupations gained workers from this effort. Those numbers decreased immediately after the war when the men returned home, but steadily increased as time passed.

2. Supplies for military troops overseas as well as military troops and civilians at home. This included timber, cotton, tobacco, food (planting, harvesting, canning, fishing), clothing, arms and ammunition, and transportation vehicles for land, sea and air.

3. Building and maintenance of new and expanded military installations as well as roads, railways, airfields, dams, and camps for POWs and enemy aliens.

Train at Utah ASF Depot, courtesy of Special Collections Department, Stewart Library, Weber State University

Global Situation

POWs held by the British and French were straining their limited supplies, so they needed to be farmed out to other Allied nations (Algeria, Australia, Canada, Egypt, Great Britain, India, Kenya, Libya, the Middle East, South Africa, and the U.S.). POWs were being held in the various theaters of war, but the numbers were much greater than could be used for supply and support behind combat lines. Great Britain held 23,000 German and 250,000 Italian prisoners in August 1942. Plans were made to transport them to places where their care would not remove men from combat and where their labor could be used to ease shortages caused by men away from home.

Generally, ships carrying supplies and men into the European and Mediterranean theaters of war were used to transport POWs back to America, Canada, Australia, etc. While many POWs worried about getting bombed or torpedoed by their own nations, there were few incidents. The SS *Benjamin Contee* was torpedoed off the coast of Algeria on August 16, 1943, by German aircraft. The ship proceeded to Bone, to Algiers and then to Gibraltar, where emergency repairs were made, then to New York City, arriving January 29, 1944. The bodies of thirty-six unidentifiable Italian prisoners (900 British-held Italian prisoners had been on this ship before the attack) were removed from the most damaged part of the vessel and buried at Long Island National Cemetery.

The German POW population in the U.S. in May 1942 was only thirty-one with one Japanese POW. There were no Italian POWs here at that time.

The Italian POWs were captured by British, French, and American troops between 1939 and 1943 in North Africa and Europe. They first arrived in the U.S. in early 1943 through the New York Port of Embarkation.

For the captured officers and naval crews, interrogation centers were their first stops in America. Fort Hunt, VA, was the first of these centers. These interrogators denied torture and criticized the Bush administration when they were honored near Alexandria as part of the U.S. Army's Freedom Team salute program in 2007. The National Park Service (NPS), particularly the George Washington Memorial Parkway which now contains the former Fort Hunt, is interviewing veterans of P.O. Box 1142 (as it was known then) to tell their story. The former interrogators include John Gunther Dean, later a career Foreign Service Officer and ambassador to Denmark who said, "We did it with a certain amount of respect and justice." George Frenkel said, "During the many interrogations, I never laid hands on anyone." He said, "We extracted information in a battle of the wits, I'm proud to say I never compromised my humanity."

Above: Vincenzo Lo Giudice is shown here with his Italian Army friends in North Africa [*Courtesy of his daughter, Carmelina*]

Below: Byron Hot Springs (CA) back door, the entrance for the POWs, Joint U.S. Army and U.S. Navy interrogation center [*Courtesy of Carol A. Jensen, historian at Byron Hot Springs*]

The second interrogation center was Byron Hot Springs CA, also known as P.O. Box 651. Following the example of the British to gain maximum cooperation with excellent living conditions, this former resort spa was used primarily for the highest-ranking German officers and Japanese naval crews while Fort Hunt was used primarily for German naval crews. Information gained at Fort Hunt and Byron Hot Springs was also used later in the murder trials of naval POWs accused of murder in the camps.

The third interrogation center appearing on the camp lists as "restricted listing," the same designation as the two locations above, has recently been exposed as Pine Grove Furnace, NY.

These interrogation centers were run by a combination of Military Intelligence, an agency of the Adjutant General's Office (G-2), and the Office of Naval Intelligence (ONI). Since this was against Geneva Convention rules, they were listed on PMGO lists of POW Camps as "restricted listing" camps to conceal their locations.

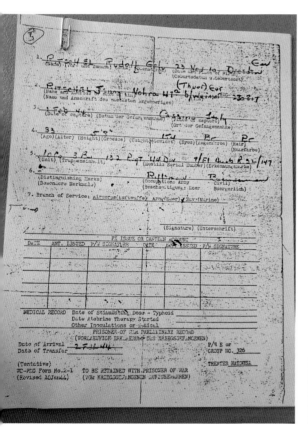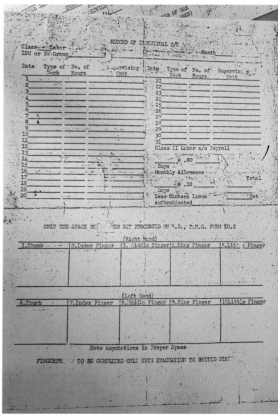

This preliminary record was kept by Rudolf Bitschel and given to Lowell Bangerter, a German professor who translated when the former POW returned to the logging camp where he lived near Dubois [*Courtesy of Steven Banks*]

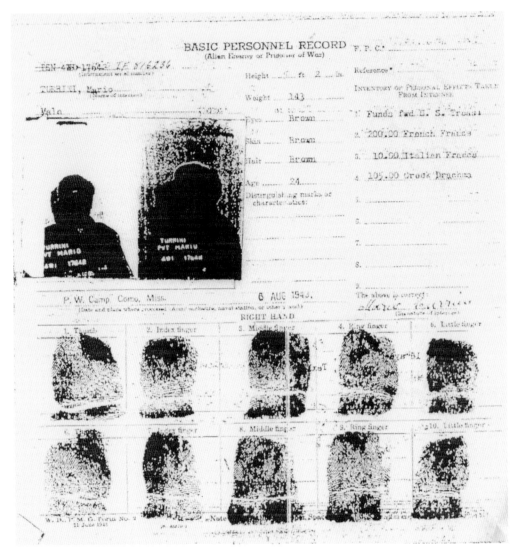

This ID card for Mario Turrini was created at Camp Como, MS. Note that the ID number was crossed out when they realized he already had a POW number assigned by the British who had originally captured him. In the far right column you can see that he had coins from France (from his service in Tunisia), plus coins from Italy (from his Italian Army pay), plus coins from Greece (his last duty station before Tunisia). [*These documents are courtesy of his son, Marcello, who lives in Italy.*]

14-NOV-2007 MER 12:13 NR. FAX P 02

1. Pvt. Army Artillery
   (Grade and arm or service)
10. May 11, 1943
    (Date of capture or arrest)

2. 3rd Rgt. Artig.
   (Hostile unit or vessel)
11. Tunisia
    (Place of capture or arrest)

3. --
   (Hostile serial number)
12. English
    (Unit or vessel making capture or arresting agency)

4. Dec. 22, 1919   Greve Inchianti Firenze
   (Date and country of birth)
13. Farmer
    (Occupation)

5. Greve Inchianti Firenze
   (Place of permanent residence)
14. Elementary School   (3 years)
    (Education)

6. Settimo Turrini Father
   (Name, relationship of nearest relative)
15. --
    (Knowledge of language)

7. Same as no. 5
   (Address of above)
16. Good
    (Physical condition at time of capture or arrest)

8. --
   (Number of dependents and relationship)
17. Single
    (Married or single)

9. --
   (Address of above)
18. Catholic
    (Religious preference)

ADDITIONAL DATA:

Transferred from	Date depart	Transferred to	Date received	Official signature of receiving officer	Personal effects not transferred
PW Camp, Ruston, La.	16 May 44	PW Camp, Hereford, Tex.			
PRISONER OF WAR CAMP HEREFORD, TEXAS	SEP 2 1944	POE SEATTLE WAS.	SEP 5 1944		
CAS SEC FT LAWTON SEP 9 1944		HAW. DEPT	SEP 16 1944		
Hq. P.O.W. Camp APO 950	JAN 17 1946			ITALY REPATRIATED	

REMARKS:

¹ If no relative, name person to be notified in case of emergency.
² If personal effects taken from individual are not transferred, note exceptions and place of storage or depot.

This card for Mario Turrini was created at Camp Ruston, LA, his location after processing at Camp Como. It shows that in May 1944 he was transferred to Camp Hereford, TX. This is part of the sorting process and he was categorized as not cooperative since he didn't sign up to be a co-belligerent in the Italian Service Units (ISU) after the fall of Mussolini. In September 1944, he was transferred to the Seattle Port of Entry, particularly Fort Lawton, from which he sailed two weeks later for duty at POW Camp APO 950, AKA Fort Armstrong, Honolulu, HI. The Italian prisoners weren't sure where they were going and there were rumors that they would be sent into combat zones in the Pacific theater.

Planning and Building the Camps

Initially, enemy alien camps were planned for 100,000 internees. However, after it was determined that original parameters for designating enemy aliens as potential threats were too broad and could not be implemented because of the vast numbers of people involved, the camps under construction were re-purposed as POW camps. They expected to fill them with POWs already captured by the British, about 100,000.

Lessons learned in WWI led to the separation of POWs (under the PMGO of the Army) and Enemy Aliens (under the INS within the Department of Justice [DOJ]). Also, in the wake of WWI were the agreements made at the Geneva Convention in 1929. It was determined that the U.S. would (usually) follow such agreements not only because of the legal obligations, but also in hopes of reciprocal good treatment by our enemies.

Among those soldiers captured in German uniform were men who considered themselves another nationality, such as Austrian, Czech, Swiss, Italian, Russian, Mongol, Hungarian, Romanian, and more. Among those captured in Japanese uniform were Koreans. Among those captured in Italian uniforms were Slavs (present day Croatia, Bosnia, and Slovenia), Albanians, and Ethiopians. It was quickly learned that these groups needed to be separated in the POW camps both at home and abroad. In many of these groups were men who claimed U.S. citizenship. Their trials were postponed repeatedly until the end of the war when they were sent back to the nation in whose army they had been captured.

Only one of the POW camps had previously been used as WWI POW camp: Fort Douglas, UT. Some were already military installations, like Fort Jay, NY. Some were former Civilian Conservation Corps (CCC) camps, like Fort Hunt, VA. Many were new purchases, like Camp Monticello, AR.

There were several potential standard camp plans, adapted to different climates and geographical considerations, but ultimately, each camp was unique in its layout due to geography and transportation infrastructure. In addition to building barracks, mess halls, warehouses, administrative buildings, and a hospital, the first commanding officer of the Utah ASF Depot POW camp, UT, designated fifty acres nearby to grow crops to help feed the POWs. The crop yield was so bountiful it was shared with the Depot cafeteria, the Depot quartermaster, Bushnell General Hospital (in Brigham City), and the Ogden Air Service Command at nearby Hill Field. A similar assortment of buildings and garden areas was described at most other base camp locations.

Above: Garden at Utah ASF Depot [*Courtesy of Special Collections Department, Stewart Library, Weber State University*]

Right: Italian Prisoners of War in freight yard at Utah ASF Depot [*Courtesy of Special Collections Department, Stewart Library, Weber State University*]

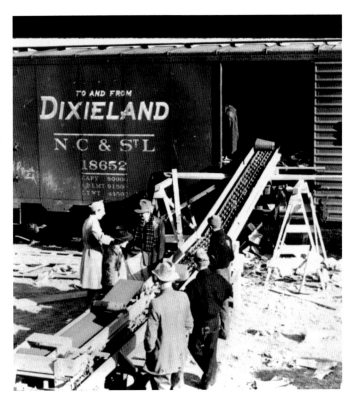

Ogden POW camp barracks [*Courtesy of Special Collections Department, Stewart Library, Weber State University*]

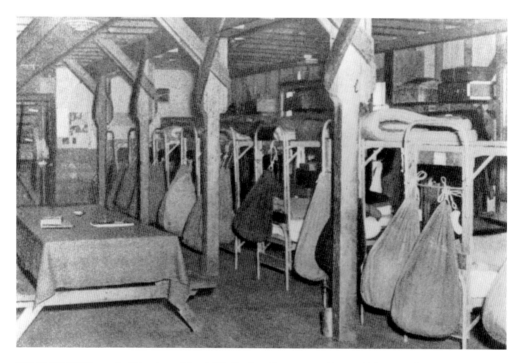

Hill Field POW barracks [*Courtesy of Special Collections Department, Stewart Library, Weber State University*]

Managing the Camps

Security was a primary concern. Guards were a combination of military (often older men and wounded combat veterans) and civilian. Sometimes long-lasting friendships developed between the guards and the POWs they watched, particularly among the interpreters.

In a successful effort to conserve manpower, it was the experience at Utah ASF Depot, UT, that one woman with a dog could patrol the same area as two men.

The POW work details were supervised by guards armed with carbines and rifles. Originally, the ratio was one guard to ten POWs, but over time diminished to one guard to thirty-two prisoners. When U.S. Army personnel was not available, the base commander could supply guards from other sources. Handcuffing or abuse was forbidden. Each of the guard towers in the compound was occupied by a guard equipped with machine guns.

Sometimes the U.S. Army translators were also guards, like Thomas M. Todaro, who worked at Camp Monticello and later at Fort Leonard Wood, MO. Translators (usually U.S. military) were assigned to camps. However, U.S. military translators for Italian Service Units (ISU) were assigned to the units which moved from camp to camp as needed to provide services.

The POWs were soon discovered to be an uneasy (sometimes dangerous) mix of several nationalities, languages, and ideologies—regardless of their uniform. They were then segregated by nationality and politics and rank. In many camps, the officers were simply held in a separate compound from the enlisted, as directed by the Geneva Convention. However, compounds at Camps Beale, Blanding, McCain, and Papago Park were designated for German Naval crews. Camp Alva was for Nazis. Camps Blanding, Campbell, and Devens were Anti-Nazi camps. Camps Hereford, Monticello, and Weingarten were for Italian fascists. These divisions into Nazi and Anti-Nazi were based on judgments made by G-2, the Army Intelligence unit.

The generalities do not take into account transfers from camp to camp that were frequent and based on additional factors, such as work, health, and relationships. Most POWs didn't accurately fall into the above categories; they were young men who grew up in societies with mandatory youth groups and mandatory military service whose families were living in Nazi-controlled locations.

After initial interrogation, the German generals were placed at Camps Clinton and Dermott while Italian generals and officers were at Camp Monticello. Additional German officers were held at Crossville.

Above: POW farmers At Camp Atterbury, IN [*Courtesy of Gary Reeves's collection of POW artifacts*]

Left: Sketch of Camp Carson guard tower [*Courtesy of Gary Reeves's collection of POW artifacts*]

POW Farm labor with guards [*Courtesy of Gary Reeves's collection of POW artifacts*]

ARMY SERVICE FORCES
NINTH SERVICE COMMAND
POST STOCKADE & PRISON OFFICE
CAMP ADAIR, OREGON

10 May 1944

SPECIAL ORDERS FOR PRISONER CHASERS

1. I will keep this order in my possession at all times while on duty as a prisoner chaser.

2. I will learn the names of prisoners assigned to me for work; and the exact location and kind of work to be done and will see that the prisoners wear their full fatigue uniforms at work.

3. I will not allow my prisoners to separate or get more than fifteen (15) paces from me, or closer than six (6) paces to me. I will keep my prisoners in sight at all times.

4. When I cannot safely guard my prisoners I will return them to the Post Stockade and report the circumstances.

5. I will not allow my prisoners to enter any building, except designated latrines, while at work.

6. I will not smoke, converse with anyone, lean against any object, sit down, discard, or lay aside my arms.

7. I will keep my prisoners constantly at work, giving them one (1) break in the morning and one (1) break in the afternoon.

8. I will immediately return my prisoners to the Post Stockade when "recall from fatigue" is sounded, or when work assigned is finished.

9. If I am ordered to escort my prisoners on a vehicle, I will post myself on one side of the vehicle with prisoners on opposite side. I will maintain a position whereby prisoners are within sight at all times, both on and off of vehicles.

10. If a prisoner attempts to escape, the sentinel or any member of the Main Guard or Prisoner Guard who sees him will call "HALT": If the prisoner fails to halt when the sentinel has repeated his call, and if there is no possible means of preventing his escape, the sentinel will fire at him. (Par. 44F / TR 135-15).

11. I will at no time allow my prisoner to congregate or mill around with other prisoners, civilians, or other soldiers.

12. I understand that I am fully responsible for the conduct, and work performed by prisoners assigned to me to guard, and that I am subject to Disciplinary action if I fail to enforce these orders properly or promptly, and report any misconduct on the part of the prisoners to the Post Prison Officer. Phone 2847.

Elliott L. Bounds
ELLIOTT L. BOUNDS
1st Lt., QMC
Police & Prison Officer

Instructions for POW guards, issued at Camp Adair (OR) [*Courtesy of Gary Reeves' collection of POW artifacts*]

Above left: This British Issue Dog Tag for an Italian enlisted POW was on display at the March Air Field Museum display on Camp Haan (CA) [*Photo by author*]

Above right: Thomas M. Todaro, guard and translator [*Courtesy of his son, Robert*]

Below: Board at Fort Devons (MA) showing those POWs who could work without a guard [*Courtesy of Gary Reeves's collection of POW artifacts*]

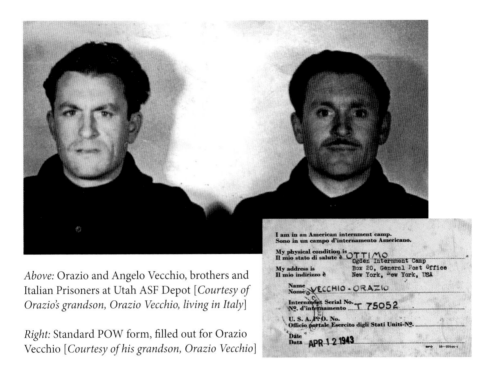

Above: Orazio and Angelo Vecchio, brothers and Italian Prisoners at Utah ASF Depot [*Courtesy of Orazio's grandson, Orazio Vecchio, living in Italy*]

Right: Standard POW form, filled out for Orazio Vecchio [*Courtesy of his grandson, Orazio Vecchio*]

G-2 interviewed these officers; however, the highest-ranking officer in these interrogation teams was a major, so not perceived by the POWs as qualified to deal with an officer of higher rank. Consequently, cursory, and sometimes erroneous conclusions were drawn, heavily influenced by other high-ranking enemy officers who were invited to participate.

A glaring example is the input of Italian General Trezzani, who used the opportunity to cast doubt (and worse, calling another Italian general a Nazi). He used this ploy on officers of similar rank to promote himself with the Americans. He used it to great advantage to become the head of the Italian Service Units (ISU) in the U.S. and later in charge of rebuilding the Italian Army in post-war Italy.

Additionally, Italian Royalists and career army were considered fascist while German career army were considered Nazi, simply for participating in youth groups (required) or in support of Franco (military service) in Spain. There was so much more to the story.

Public opinion was most loudly expressed by those with the greatest fear of enemy camps in their towns, or by those who hoped to profit from the use of POW labor in their businesses. Most Americans viewed the new camps with caution, but acceptance, and gradually came to appreciate the additional civilian jobs and affordable labor source. Some even developed friendships which lasted long after the war ended.

Each prisoner was processed either when captured or when they arrived in the U.S. This process included searching, delousing, disinfecting, fumigation, bathing, registration, clothing issue, quartering, and medical inspection.

Above: Giovanni D'Onofrio (third from left) and POW friends at Utah ASF Depot [*Courtesy of his children, Vincent, Orazio, and Janice*]

Below: Carlo Selmi and POW friends at Utah ASF Depot [*Courtesy of his son, Andrea, living in Italy*]

6

Life in the Camps

The maximum number of German POWs held in the Continental U.S. was 371,683 in May 1945. Italian POWs (Continental U.S.) reached a maximum of 51,156 in November 1944. Japanese POWs (Continental U.S.) reached a maximum of 5413 in August 1945. There were POW Camps in every state except Vermont, plus the territories of Hawaii and Alaska.

The POWs were placed into companies of 250 men each, 8 companies to a compound (2000 men), with two compounds at Ogden ASF Depot in 1943. Later, one compound at Ogden ASF Depot was composed of Italian Service Units while the other housed German POWs who were willing to work there. They were the first camp to work the two groups together, with Germans supervising Italians and the opposite.

Each base camp had a station hospital, staffed by both Americans and POWs. Utah ASF Depot station hospital had 100 beds, like most station hospitals. Since many POWs arrived in poor health due to long imprisonment and poor diet (both before and after imprisonment), that hospital admitted over 2000 men by June 1944 after opening only 18 months earlier.

Housing and furnishings at first met, and then exceeded the Geneva Convention requirements. Since the camps were in different locations, some utilized barracks, some hutments (smaller housing units) while the temporary and seasonal camps often used tents. The Geneva Convention required mattresses only for officers. Eventually, most permanent camps had mattresses, pillows and pillowcases on iron and wooden beds for enlisted men as well as officers.

General Hospitals, run by the Surgeon General of Army Service Forces (ASF), were in each region, utilizing a POW wing to facilitate security. In 1944, they became more specialized to receive all patients from theaters of operations, plus patients needing specialized treatment in the Zone of Interior.

Those station hospitals with airfields were overseen by the Air Surgeon of the Army Air Force (AAF). In 1944, Regional Hospitals (a new designation), station hospitals, and convalescent centers were now run by both the ASF and AAF. The Regional Hospitals were to serve as General Hospitals for Zone of Interior patients. These designations are rarely mentioned in the population lists in the National Archives.

The station hospitals were generally staffed with an American officer of the Medical Corps and 3 POW attendants with medical training. The surgical staff included an American Medical Officer, a nurse, an enlisted man and 3 POW attendants with medical training. POWs also served as lab technicians. The hospital mess was under the mess officer with a civilian nurse and a mess sergeant. It was staffed by two U.S. Army mess sergeants, 1 POW mess sergeant and 4 POW cooks. Provisions were made for special diets.

Mental patients in Utah were sent to Bushnell General Hospital, UT while extreme cases were sent to Mason General Hospital, NY. Dental care was also provided at the station hospitals for the POWs treating abscesses, and doing extractions, fillings, and gum treatments. At Utah ASF Depot, over 17,000 dental cases were treated during the year of 1943-1944.

Upon arrival, the POWs were issued clothing and blankets which were maintained and replaced as needed. The Red Cross in New York was issuing two pairs of blankets per man and a uniform that might be the dark blue with white PW lettering, or an old U.S. Army uniform, plus the uniform he arrived wearing. Not many had overcoats, some came with English overcoats, black with a black diamond on the back.

The POWs were supposed to be adequately, comfortably, and properly clothed in accordance with the climate conditions in which they lived and worked according to the Geneva Convention of 1929. The War Department later determined that dark blue was a preferable uniform color since it would not be mistaken for the American khaki. They were also provided with woolen underwear, cotton underwear, woolen socks and cotton socks, woolen shirts and cotton shirts, two pairs of trousers in either wool or denim, two cotton coats in wool or khaki, a wool overcoat, a raincoat, woolen caps and hats, cotton hats and caps, shoes and overshoes, gloves, and two heavy woolen blankets. When an item wore out, it was immediately replaced. The clothing was class X or Class B, American issue.

Some camps had laundry facilities with machines while some had wash rooms where laundry was done by hand.

Education included classes in English, history, and democracy plus clerical and equipment training. Supplies were provided for many art projects and newsletter production.

Newspapers were produced by the prisoners at most of the larger camps. There is a collection of Italian POW newsletters at Utah State University. There is a large collection of German POW newsletters at the Library of Congress. Many of these newsletters can be found at local colleges and historical societies.

Camp Carson German POWs published Die PW Wolke. Camp Greeley German POWs published Ratsel Humor, full of puzzles and cartoons. Greeley German POWs also published Deutsche Kriegsfenangenschaft: Colorado - Amerika 1944-45 for more literary and sentimental work.

Their food was the equivalent of that issued to American servicemen (type A field ration), according to the Geneva Convention, although substitutions were made to recognize ethnic preferences. The Italian POWs had an increase in rice, spaghetti, macaroni, noodles and pasta with decreases in meats and baked beans. Germans had an increase in potatoes and a decrease in beans. Meals were served 3 times daily. Special menus were prepared on Thanksgiving, Christmas, New Year's and other holidays. For many prisoners, these rations exceeded their military experience. The average prisoner at Utah ASF Depot gained 15 pounds.

Utah ASF Depot Hospital grounds [*Courtesy of Special Collections Department, Stewart Library, Weber State University*]

Utah ASF Depot Hospital steps [*Courtesy of Special Collections Department, Stewart Library, Weber State University*]

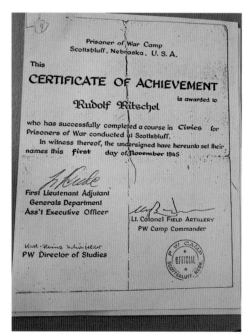

Above: Utah ASF Depot POW Class with civilian instructor and U.S. Army guard [*Courtesy of Special Collections Department, Stewart Library, Weber State University*]

Left: Certificates were given to the POWs who completed a variety of courses in the camps. This achievement in civics was awarded to Rudolf Ritschel and given to Lowell Bangerter, a German professor who translated when the former POW returned to the logging camp where he lived in Dubois (WY) [*Courtesy of Steven Banks*]

Above left: POW Newspaper from Fort McClellan, AL [[*Courtesy of Gary Reeves's collection of POW artifacts*]]

Above right: Some beautiful art was created in the camps; this piece from Colorado shows a sense of humor as well [*Courtesy of Gary Reeves's collection of POW artifacts*]

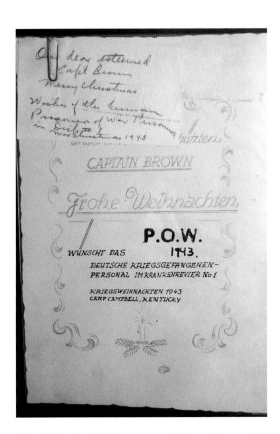

Above left and right: Christmas card from a German POW at Camp Campbell (KY) [*Courtesy of Gary Reeves's collection of POW artifacts*]

Above: Italian POW cooks at Utah ASF Depot [*Courtesy of Special Collections Department, Stewart Library, Weber State University*]

Below: Utah ASF Depot Italian POW Bakery [*Courtesy of Special Collections Department, Stewart Library, Weber State University*]

The POWs were their own cooks and bakers, paid the same wage as those working in all occupations both in and outside of the camps. However, each camp commander had some autonomy and after the liberation of concentration camps in Germany, some camps restricted food allowances for POWs well below Geneva Convention (Hereford, TX is infamous for it's dietary cuts in 1945).

Many services were available for POWs, some in accord with the Geneva Convention and some additional benefits. They included Canteens, camp stores where a POW could spend the pay (in coupons) he earned working on such items as beer, cigarettes, and gold jewelry (high quality necklaces, wedding rings and rosaries were in high demand by the Italian POWs at Utah ASF Depot). The profits from the sales were returned to the POWs in the form of free beer, cigarettes, and theater tickets.

Some POW photos show the decorations (pin-ups) in their personal areas. These could include small pictures of national leaders and flags and emblems, but large displays were limited to funerals and religious services.

Recreation supplies were provided for many sports, although soccer was most popular. Other equipment included baseball, softball, basketball, football, boxing, volleyball, croquet, horse shoes, badminton, and table tennis. Many game sets were also provided for the POWs including dominoes, Chinese checkers, checkers, backgammon, India, bingo, chess, playing cards, etc. The POW often constructed their own volleyball courts, baseball diamonds and soccer fields.

Above left: Ration coupons were issued by each camp, but the format was standardized as shown here of coupons from Camp Livingston (LA), Camp Grant (IL), and Camp Rupert (ID) [*Courtesy of Gary Reeves's collection of POW artifacts*]

Above right: This photo was taken for a news service of the Canteen at Camp Custer (MI) [*Courtesy of Gary Reeves's collection of POW artifacts*]

Above: This photo shows the distribution of cigarettes to POW at one of the camps [*Courtesy of Gary Reeves's collection of POW artifacts*]

Below left: Matchbooks were made for Fort Robinson (NE) and many other camps [*Courtesy of Gary Reeves's collection of POW artifacts*]

Below right: Some camps issued cards for special items, like this Beer Card [*Courtesy of Gary Reeves's collection of POW artifacts*]

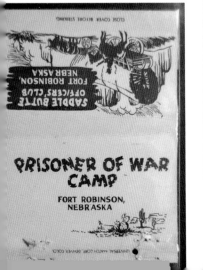

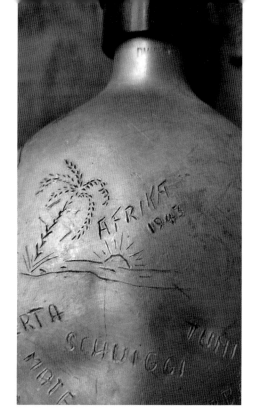

Above: Of course, people create art out of whatever is available, as evidenced by this water canteen with inscriptions from this German soldier's time in Africa in 1943 [*Courtesy of Gary Reeves's collection of POW artifacts*]

Below: Barracks at Camp Atterbury (IN) [*Courtesy of Alessandro de Gaetano*]

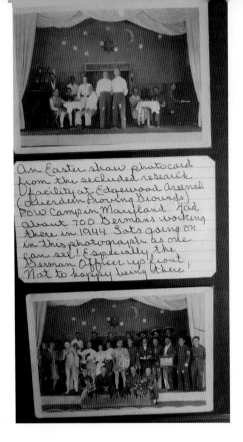

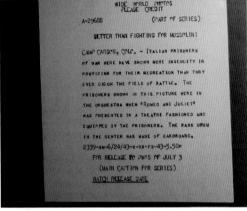

Above left: Theatrical productions were part of the recreation at each camp. This was at Edgewood Arsenal, MD [*Courtesy of Gary Reeves's collection of POW artifacts*]

Above right: Camp Carson musicians with cardboard bass drum [*Courtesy of Gary Reeves's collection of POW artifacts*]

Left: POW Soccer Team at Edgewood Arsenal (MD) [*Courtesy of Gary Reeves's collection of POW artifacts*]

POW contacts with families and others included inspection visits from the Red Cross, YMCA, Swiss government and other welfare organizations. Each POW was permitted two letters and one post card per week, written in ink (not pencil). Also, when necessary, one business letter per week. Special stationary was provided, so limited to the lines on the forms. Free mailing was applied to all letters, postcards, and parcels less than four pounds, addressed to or sent by a POW through the U.S. Postal Service. Each POW was also allowed, at his own expense, one prepaid cable or telegram per month. In the event of a serious emergency (death or serious illness), and at the discretion of the base commander, more than one per month may be sent.

Incoming mail for Italian POWs from relatives in the U.S. was enormous. In two or three months alone, 300-500 packages were received at Utah ASF Depot. The POWs sent many gifts to their relatives in this country and to those outside the Continental U.S. Correspondence to POWs was permitted from anyone. However, POWs could only write to and receive packages from family members such as wives, grandparents, parents, siblings, aunts, uncles, children, nieces, and nephews.

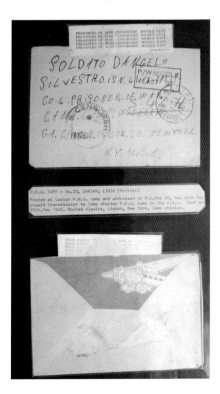 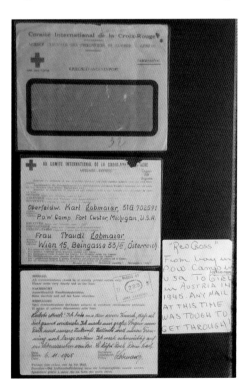

Above left: This letter was sent from a British POW camp in Garian (Libya) to a POW in Camp Wheeler, GA [*Courtesy of Gary Reeves's collection of POW artifacts*]

Above right: This letter was sent through the Red Cross from a POW Camp in Custer (MI) to a young woman in Austria. Some letters were also sent through the Vatican as an alternative to the U.S. mail. [*Courtesy of Gary Reeves's collection of POW artifacts*]

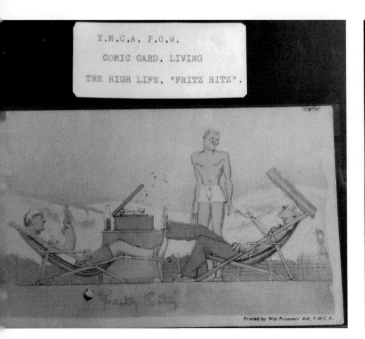

Above left: This postcard was designed by a German POW and printed by the YMCA [*Courtesy of Gary Reeves's collection of POW artifacts*]

Above right: Postcard with a group photo of German POWs [*Courtesy of Gary Reeves's collection of POW artifacts*]

Below: Many camps and military installations had their own postcards [*Courtesy of Robert Todaro from his father's duty assignment there as a POW translator and guard*]

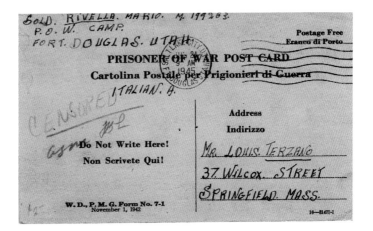

POW Postcard from Fort Douglas (UT) [*Courtesy of Dennis H. Pack*]

Acrobats on stage at Fort Lewis (WA) [*Courtesy of Gary Reeves's collection of POW artifacts*]

ISU Band at Utah USF Depot [*Courtesy of Andrea Selmi, son of Carlo Selmi, clarinet player in this band (third from left), living in Italy*]

Most camps had bands and/or orchestras made up of their POW population. At many locations, concerts were held once a week. The orchestras also played for stage shows and gave monthly concerts. Many instruments were provided by the Catholic church, others were loaned by the Depot Quartermaster. At some camps, the local schools and communities provided instruments.

The ISU band at Utah ASF Depot played for dances each week, both at the POW Camp and at St. Joseph's Catholic Church in Ogden. The dances were a good place to meet the local girls. The POWs were taken to the church by bus from the camp. Separate dances (different nights) for officers and enlisted POWs to adhere to Geneva Convention.

Religion was also a part of camp life. At first, religious services at Ogden, UT were held in the open with an improvised pulpit. Later, a recreation hall was used part time for morning Mass. An empty barrack was utilized as a regular chapel for weekdays. Later, the old Compound One Headquarters building became the Main Chapel and accommodated about 300 POWs for daily Mass. When Compound Two was activated, one of its recreational halls was provided for chapel functions and accommodated about 700. This camp was Italian, so only Catholic services were required. The hospital also held Mass on Sunday. When the camp opened a German compound, a Lutheran minister provided services on Sunday in addition to the Catholic services for the German POWs. Every U.S. camp had a similar regard for religious services.

While POWs weren't allowed to donate blood (prohibited by the PMGO and Geneva Convention), they were allowed to make voluntary contributions to specific organizations, such as the Red Cross and the YMCA. A minor political group at Utah ASF Depot, the Republicans, collected $80 for

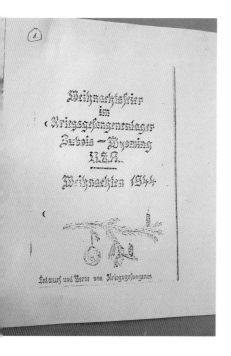

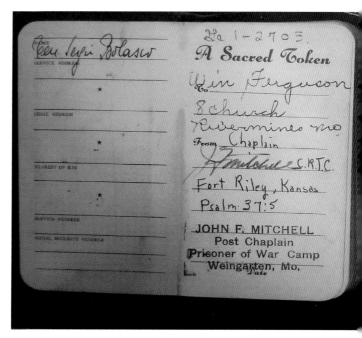

Above left: Christmas program at Camp Dubois by and for the German POWs [*Courtesy of Steven Banks*]

Above right: This Bible seems to have gone from Win Ferguson to Italian Lt. Sergei Bolasco after being presented by a U.S. Army Chaplain who served at both Fort Riley (KS) and POW Camp Weingarten (MO), [*Courtesy of Gary Reeves's collection of POW artifacts*]

Right: Madonna made and placed at Camp Lockett (CA) near their housing area by Italian POWs [*Courtesy of Mountain Empire Historical Society*]

war bonds, offered to donate blood, and offered money to the Infantile Paralysis Fund because they believed it was a good cause.

Escapes were expected and did occur at several locations. Most of them were short in duration and distance, usually ending with an easy capture or surrender since the object was just to get outside the fence for a while. Some were more serious, with bigger plans and groups of men, also usually ending in surrender. Just a few men were able to remain at large until many years after the war ended. No reports of sabotage or terrorism were ever associated with these escapes.

At Fruita, 3 German POWs escaped while harvesting beets, but were re-captured the next morning when caught sleeping in a haystack by a local boy who called the authorities.

Three German POWs left the Rocky Mountain Arsenal Camp to be caught by a state trooper who found them walking down the highway toward Denver.

A tunnel at Trinidad enabled many escapes. It was 150 feet long, 5 feet high, and 30 inches wide. It ended 65 feet beyond the reach of the searchlight outside the camp. The entrance was in the German officers' compound.

On 16 October 1943, four German POWs used the tunnel with maps and supplies provided by five Japanese-American sisters who worked on the same farm. Among the supplies were photos of the men with the women, found when the men were re-captured in New Mexico. Those photos were later published in the Denver Post with sensational headlines. The Associated Press circulated the photos, promoting stories about "Japanazi Romances", an embarrassment to the authorities who had imprisoned them. At the time, the photo of a kiss suggested sex between our enemies and miscegenation. Although the men denied that the women's actions were treasonous and even spoke on their behalf (while witnesses for the prosecution) at their trial for treason. The POWs claimed that the women tried to talk them out of the escape attempt and the men seduced them into cooperating in the escape. The women were convicted of "conspiracy to commit treason" and sentenced to serve time in a federal prison for women in West Virginia. The limited sentences for the three sisters convicted (20-24 months) seem to confirm that the court didn't support the treason charge, but felt the need to take action. The last woman was released in 1946, about the same time other Japanese-Americans were released from their Relocation Centers.

Along with 100,000 other Japanese-Americans, their family had been relocated. They were sent to the Granada War Relocation Center, also known as Camp Amache. About a year later, they were sent to harvest onions near Trinidad. A section of the town of Trinidad was used for the interned Japanese Americans and even had it's own post office which you can see from the postcard image in this book.

Captain Till Edward Kiefer was the most famous escapee from Trinidad, captured at St. Louis in his Nazi uniform (although dyed brown) in the train station. That was his second of three escapes from American POWs camps, re-captured all three times. After the war, he became an actor in Hollywood under the name Til Kiwe. Ironically, he played a German guard in "The Great Escape" who shot at Steve McQueen as he emerged from the escape tunnel.

The most famous Colorado POW was Rüdiger Freiherr von Wechmar, a baron and officer of the Africa Korp, later bacame the Federal Republic of Germany's ambassador to the U.N. and in 1980 the president of the General Assembly.

Two German POWs escaped from Camp Hale, driven to the Mexican border by Dale Maple, an American Nazi sympathizer assigned to the 620th General Engineering Corps with other men of questionable loyalty, stationed at Camp Hale. The three were captured 3 miles inside Mexico by a Mexican border agent. Maple was convicted of treason and sentenced to death, but President Roosevelt commuted the sentence to life imprisonment. The sentence was further commuted to 10 years after 17 months.

There was public concern about escapes, prompting the Army to compile a Congressional report stating the the escape rate from Federal Prisons was .44 of 1 percent while the escape rate from POW camps (with fewer guards and safety measures) was .45 of 1 percent.

There were pets among the POWs, sometimes traveling with them from POW Camp to POW Camp.

These newspaper photos showed the shocking close relations between German POWs and Japanese-American women [*Courtesy of Gary Reeves's collection of POW artifacts*]

Above: These newspaper photos showed the prosecution team at the treason trial of three Japanese-American women [*Courtesy of Gary Reeves's collection of POW artifacts*]

Left: Til Kiwe, a POW who escaped from three camps and was later an actor in Hollywood [*Photo from ww2. gravestone.com*]

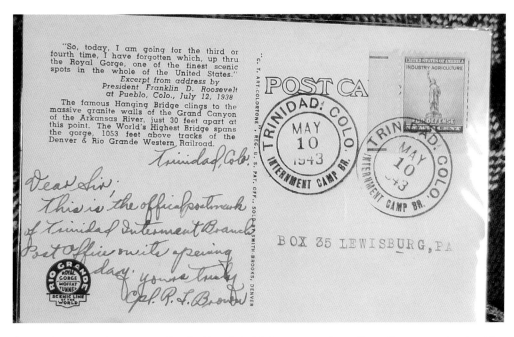

Above: This postcard was stamped at the Trinidad, CO Internment Camp Post office on opening day, May 10, 1943 [*Courtesy of Gary Reeves's collection of POW artifacts*]

Below: A group of Italian POWs at Camp Lockett, CA, pose with their priest and their dog [*Courtesy of Mountain Empire Historical Society*]

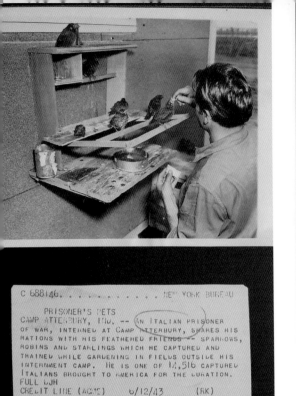

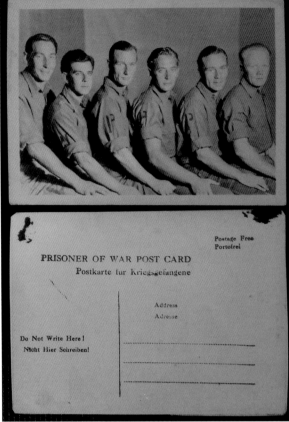

Above left: This photo of a POW with pet birds outside the barracks was taken at Camp Atterbury made the national newsreels [*Courtesy of Gary Reeves's collection of POW artifacts*]

Above right: Postcard with a group photo of German POWs [*Courtesy of Gary Reeves's collection of POW artifacts*]

Below: In 1953, *Colliers Magazine* published a story about five German POW still missing. One escaped from near Bastrop (LA), one from Las Cruces (NM), one from Fort Dix (NJ), one from Deming (NM) and one from Camp Butner (NC) [*Courtesy of Gary Reeves's collection of POW artifacts*]

POW work included occupations required for the maintenance of the camps, such as cooking, cleaning, clothing and shoe repairs, landscaping, etc.

They also were hired out for canning and farming in the community, including pruning orchards and planting as well as harvesting. They also worked on dams, railroads, orchards, mining, quarrying, and forestry. The businesses and farmers paid the government a minimum wage and the POWs were paid 80 cents a day, comparable to the wage for a civilian day laborer.

Even the Ogden Chamber of Commerce hired POWs, and Italian POWs at Fort Monmouth, NJ were making violins.

Other POWs were working on occupations labeled military, such as at hospitals, supply offices, post exchanges, construction, dying uniforms, landscaping, and woodworking.

Sometimes POWs worked on community service projects outside the camp. The Catholic Church of St. Mary's in Umbarger, TX was beautifully decorated with murals and other artwork by Italian POWs from nearby Camp Hereford.

Murals painted by Italian POWs at St. Mary's Catholic Church at Umbarger (TX) [*Courtesy of John Saffell*]

A Papal Delegate visited the Italian POWs at Camp Weingarten (MO) [*Courtesy of Gary Reeves's collection of POW artifacts*]

Clearly, this isn't the first time the folks in town have seen POWs going past; the boy on a bicycle isn't even looking at them, and the teenage girls are interested spectators [*Courtesy of Gary Reeves's collection of POW artifacts*]

Certificate of Credit Balance
for
Prisoner of War

Date 15 July 1945
Datum

This is to certify that Drexler,Otto   Cpl. 3IG 202 474 :
(PW Name)   (Rank)   (ISN)
a prisoner of war in custody of the United States of America on this date.
has a credit balance of ____ten 97/100____ $ __10.97__
(Words)   (Amount in figures)
for pay, allowances and other moneys credited to his individual account
during the period of his internment.

Bescheinigung ueber Guthaben von Kriegsgefangenen

Ich bescheinige hiermit dass Drexler,Otto   Obergefreiter
(Name des Kriegsgefangenen)   (Rang)
3IG 202 474 , Kriegsgefangener im Gewahrsam der Vereinigten Staaten von
(ISN)
Amerika, ein persoenliches Guthaben im Betrage von __Zehn 97/100__
(in Worten)
$ __10.97__ aus Sold, Zuschlaegen und sonstigen waehrend der Gefangen-
(in Zahlen)
schaft erhaltenen Geldsummen bestehend, besitzt.

LOUIS BURMAN
(Signature of Certifying Officer)
(Unterschrift des die Bescheinigung
ausstellenden Offiziers)

1st Lt.,CAC, PW Pers. Officer
(Rank and Title)
(Rang und Amt)

McAlester,Okla.
(Station)
(Dienststelle)

The above statement includes all moneys due me from the United States
of America on this date.

Die obige Bescheinigund schliesst saemtliche Geldsummen ein, die mir
gegenwaertig von der Regierung der Vereinigten Staaten zustehen.

(Prisoner of War)
(Kriegsgefangener)

WD AGO FORM 19-70   1720—SAABFD—6-6-45—70,000   THIS FORM SUPERSEDES W.D., P.M.G. FORM NO. 199, 4EDITED,
2 MAY 45   WHICH WILL NOT BE USED AFTER RECEIPT OF THIS REVISION.

This form from Camp McAlester (OK) shows the accounting made by the U.S. Army when the POWs were processed to return home [*Courtesy of Gary Reeves's collection of POW artifacts*]

The POWs were paid a minimum wage consistent with civilian day laborers if they did work (about $30/month for enlisted) or $24 a month for officers who weren't allowed to work. Those men who did work were paid $.80-1.20 each day depending on if working for local farmers or private companies. This was paid to them in coupons they could use at the Canteen, although ISU members could receive1/3 of their pay in cash to use in town. ISU members also received pay that was slightly higher (sometimes $1.50/day) to match the pay of American soldiers. That rate of pay was based on their rank in the ISU, not their Italian Army rank. An office of the Italian Army which made sure all the former POWs received their due pay was opened at the end of the war and continued until very recently. I worked in their offices in 2004 and was able to obtain records of transfers from camp to camp and the health record for a POW (with authorization from his son).

Geneva Convention required that officers be separated from enlisted men. They were sometimes in a compound next to the enlisted men and had otherwise the same types of facilities.

7

Italian Service Units

The fall of Mussolini and resultant change in that government's position in the war from Axis to Allied required some changes regarding Italian POWs. It was quickly determined that releasing them would not be the best solution. The original idea of Italian POWs being organized into units to provide labor similar to the Civilian Conservation Corps (CCC) was first proposed by the U.S. Secretary of War in October 1943. This would require separation of fascist Italian POWs from those willing to work for the war effort as co-belligerents.

They would be:

> ... attached to and placed under the command of the U.S. Army. Therefore, the plan included these features: (1) Italian prisoners would be organized into numbered Italian service companies consisting of 5 officers and 177 enlisted men ... (4) An Italian service unit headquarters would be established under ASF and would be commanded by an American officer ... The new plan provided for Italian Service Units (ISUs) to be organized from volunteer Italian PW officers, non-commissioned officers, and enlisted men under approved tables of organization and equipment, less weapons. Initially, two U.S. Army officers and 10 enlisted men were to be attached to each unit for supervision; but these were to be reduced, consistent with efficiency and security, to a minimum of one officer and five enlisted men.

The ranking Italian General over the new ISU on January 26, 1944, Claudio Trezzani, stated, "The units should be commanded by Italian officers, in this proportion; one first or second lieutenant for 30 to 35 enlisted men (platoon), one captain for 4 platoons (company), one senior officer for 3 companies (battalion), one colonel for 3 battalions (regiment)."

That letter is followed in the Italian Army file at Stato Maggiore Esercito in Rome by an apparent American response with no name or date attached, stating, "It is contemplated organizing Italian Service Units according to American tables of organization with Italian military personnel in all authorized positions, American officers and enlisted men in the smallest possible numbers will be attached as custodians, for liaison, to issue operational directives, sign payrolls and charges, and have general responsibility for the units to higher American authority."

Italian Generals Frattini and De Simone were moved to ISU headquarters at Fort Wadsworth from Camp Monticello.

Above: Italian Service Units at Utah ASF Depot [*Courtesy of Special Collections Department, Stewart Library, Weber State University*]

Below: Italian Service Unit English Class at Camp Warren (WY) [*Courtesy of Gary Reeves's collection of POW artifacts*]

The ISU program was under the command of Brig. General J. M. Eager, from the PMGO. The ASF retained the responsibilities of plans, policies, and procedures as well as the designation and strength of units and training programs and doctrines. Each unit had American personnel of one officer and five enlisted men at a minimum. Service commands were responsible for all other ISU functions and activities. Interviews with former translators assigned to those units confirmed that one American NCO was a translator for the unit.

The ISU had increased responsibilities resulting in increased privileges for the 65% of Italian POWs who signed up to serve in Italian Service Units. The new units were activated progressively with 600 POWs organized in the first week of March 1944; 1,000 for the first two weeks of April; 3,000 the third week in April; and 4,000 each succeeding week until completed. While a letter was sent to the camps from Badoglio in Rome, it was vague and general, and the Italian king never spoke (wrote) on the subject. This left many men in confusion as to the best course of action. Their families were in German-occupied Italy and many feared repercussions for such a visible support of their former enemy. The screening from ISU to POW and reverse was continuous to insure that only the most cooperative POWs were allowed the privileges of the ISU.

Those men who signed the agreement to join the ISU were given new positions and units and now lived in separate compounds than the POWs who didn't sign the agreement.

Those POWs who didn't join the ISU were classified as fascist. Instruction in English was stressed in these new units, while the same housing and wages applied, with the addition of 10 cents a day for a gratuitous allowance, sometimes more depending on the work and on their ranks in the new units. Two-thirds of the wage was paid in coupons and one-third in cash. Rules against fraternization between members of ISU and American military did not apply. ISU Service Clubs were created to give them greater access to reading materials and a quiet place to relax since they did not have access to the U.S. Army clubs. Dances and other special events were organized through the ISU Service Clubs.

Training programs for ISU was the same as for American personnel on similar jobs, with less tactics and weapons training.

Work restrictions imposed by Geneva Convention were lifted with the consent of the Badoglio government of Italy, except for combat, work at ports of embarkation within Continental U.S., and work with explosives. Their efforts released U.S. personnel for overseas duties and helped to bring about the successful conclusion of the war.

ISU units began to ship to the European theater to assist with support and supply from Africa and into Italy as part of the Liberation of Italy in the following theaters of operation: North Africa, Eastern Europe, and the Mediterranean. Apparently, some of these units were moved overseas at the discretion of the ISU command and the PMGO did not always include those units in their reports.

Mail restrictions were reduced to the same standards as American personnel for domestic correspondence. Regulations were the same as POWs for international mail. The new ISU uniforms were the same khaki as U.S. uniforms, with a patch (Italy) on the left shoulder. At least one man was court martialed for removing the Italian patch on a night out on the town,

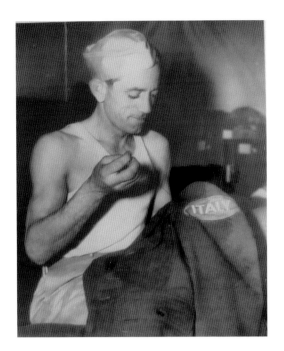

Above left: Sewing on his new ISU patch at Fort Wayne (MI) [*Courtesy of Gary Reeves's collection of POW artifacts*]

Above right: Official photos were taken of the men in their new uniforms. Note that this photo of Vincenzo Lo Giudice, provided by his daughter Carmelina, does not yet have patches for rank attached.

Below: Italian Service Club at Utah ASF Depot [*Courtesy of Special Collections Department, Stewart Library, Weber State University*]

leading to accusations of being AWOL. However, he was simply reprimanded instead of sent to a POW camp.

The POWs and their employers and guards weren't supposed to fraternize. But, of course they did. While some of the initial contact was antagonistic, many friendships and romances resulted. The ISU members did not have those restrictions, often enabling closer relationships.

ISU men were permitted weekend passes when signed out by a sponsor. Many Italian communities utilized these privileges to give some of the ISU men a family gathering, social activity, or dance. Some of the dances at the ISU Service Club included invitations to young women in the community.

Additionally, ISU members were given day passes into town for movies, dances, and just sightseeing. In Ogden, buses were used to transport ISU men from their barracks to St. Joseph's Catholic church in downtown Ogden for dances. Of course, the greatest attraction was meeting and dancing with American girls.

Some of these meetings resulted in marriages. The POWs couldn't marry, but once engaged, and returned (by June 1946), the troop transports bringing GIs home were taking these women with their escorts to Italy with the proper paperwork to marry so they could return to the U.S. with their new husbands. Several of these couples settled in the locations where they had been imprisoned, met sweethearts, and had friends.

Some of these meetings had unhappy endings. The local culture was against marrying a man of a different ethnic or religious background, plus some families feared that their girls would follow the men to Italy and never return. So those romances were discouraged, even after they created children. Some of those children were adopted out, while some stayed with their mothers who married other men in the U.S. after the war. Some of those children are sought their Italian families all their lives. Fortunately, we have assisted with some happy reunions.

Public opinion varied as shown in a variety of newspapers from those years. There were some escapes, usually associated with meeting a girl outside the camp for reasons that had nothing to do with national security.

The Italian POWs held a unique position as both POWs and Allies that created different experiences for them than for their German counterparts. In Colorado and other ISU locations, these differences meant more opportunities to not only work with the residents, but also to socialize with them. The resulting friendships (and some marriages) show the very positive results of their experiences under very difficult circumstances.

8

Death in the Camps

There were a total of 1,074 burials—including 880 Germans (includes three Russians, four Austrians, one Yugoslavian, one Czech, and one Turk), 172 Italians, twenty-three Japanese, and one Korean—out of the 1,076 POWs who died while held in the U.S. during World War II.

Many of the larger camps had their own cemeteries. After the war, the cemeteries from those camps which had been closed, and some other locations, were moved to national cemeteries to provide the perpetual care demanded by the Geneva Convention.

While most of the headstones were standard issue for U.S. military, there are some exceptions. At Fort Douglas, Eilert's stone was put up by the POWs with the permission of the camp commander and paid for by the POWs. The funeral services were often attended by Americans as well as POWs, sometimes also a POW choir and/or band, and a symbolic series of shots were fired by a military guard.

Rumors insist that most of the POWs who died here were shipped home. The truth is that the U.S. Government was willing to ship them, if the family bore the cost. Of course, most of the families were simply unable to bear that burden at the end of a war they lost. Only one Italian, Renato Facchini, was returned to Italy before February 1947, while Francesco Erriquez was returned to Italy in 2011. Apparently, none of the Germans were returned since the names in the original reports match the current cemetery records.

Some of the deaths were accidents in the course of work or recreation. Others were later deemed murders by Nazi extremists. Some were suicides, particularly at the end of the war.

There was unrest among the African-American units at Fort Lawton because they were segregated from the other U.S. soldiers, but the Italian POWs were allowed to shop in the Post Exchange with those from non-African-American units. So, when one of the Italian POWs was found strangled by hanging, three African-American soldiers were convicted of murder and another forty convicted of rioting. While none were executed, all received discharges for bad conduct which negatively affected the rest of their lives. They were finally exonerated in 2007, primarily because of the excellent research proving their innocence in *On American Soil* by Jack Hamann in 2005. Hamann also raises a suspicion that Olivotto was murdered by a U.S. Army guard who was court martialed for not being at his post during the time of the death.

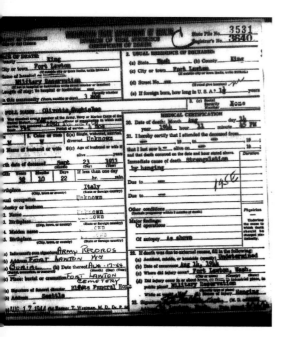
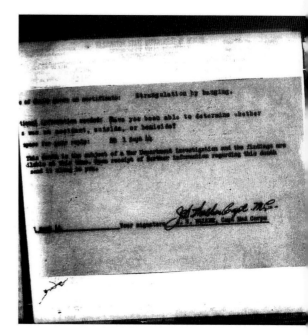

Above: Note that the cause of death for Guglielmo Olivotto shows strangulation by hanging, but whether by murder or suicide is undetermined. [*Death Certificates from Washington State Archives*]

Below: This funeral was held at Camp Monticello, AR [*Photo courtesy of Robert Todaro*]

Above: The military honor guard with rifles for a military salute at a funeral at Camp Swift (TX) [*Courtesy of Gary Reeves's collection of POW artifacts*]

Right: Death cards were printed by the family back home in Germany and Italy. This one is for a man who died at Glendon (MN), a temporary camp under Camp Algona (IA). Someone thoughtfully attached a photo of his headstone located at Fort Riley (KS) , [*Courtesy of Gary Reeves's collection of POW artifacts*]

9

Returning Home

The end of the war was cause for celebration for the POWs who could now look forward to returning home. Their newsletters often contained cartoons expressing these feelings.

Certain camps were designated as separation centers (like Haan, CA) and the POWs were moved through them, then on to ports of embarkation on both coasts for the trip home. The first returned were the Italian officers as co-belligerents. The next group was the ISU members, then the rest.

The Geneva Convention of 1929 required that POWs be returned home at the end of a war. However, the large numbers provided some logistics problems. Generally, troop ships bringing U.S. troops home turned around full of POWs. However, treaties with all countries provided that some of the POWs (not ISU) were returned to France, the USSR, and Great Britain to assist with reconstruction efforts. Some of the men in Great Britain and France worked there as long as four years before returning home. The USSR finally released the surviving prisoners ten years later.

Warnings were made regarding German POWs scheduled to be returned to their families and homes in the USSR. It was only after the first group was killed on the dock by the crew of the Soviet vessel which met them that other arrangements were made for those men.

Some POWs claimed status as U.S. citizens and requested permission to stay, but were returned to avoid the legal complications.

Some locations requested that their POWs stay long enough to complete the fall harvest and that was permitted when it could be arranged. The last POWs were repatriated (out of the U.S.) by June 30, 1946, except 141 Germans, twenty Italians, and one Japanese serving sentences in U.S. Penal Institutions. Two Germans were not repatriated; they revealed themselves many years later, perhaps more since none are shown as missing on PMGO reports.

Beyond work, Camp Carson was the location of ninety-seven sporting events and eighteen concerts with ninety-nine musicians in February 1946 alone. These activities kept the men busy while they awaited their turn to sail home.

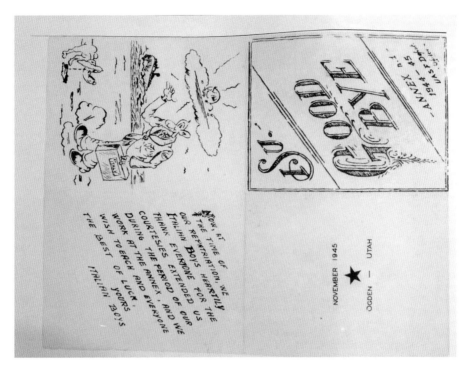

Above: This Good Bye note from the Italian Boys at Utah ASF Depot was saved by Mario Saggese, one of those boys, and used here courtesy of his daughter, living in the United States.

Below: The broken barbed wire and discarded items of entertainment show that while their time as prisoners is ended, so is their leisure time since they now need to rebuild their homes and families [*Courtesy of Gary Reeves's collection of POW artifacts*]

Above: This cartoon showing the camp for sale is much more lighthearted [*Courtesy of Gary Reeves's collection of POW artifacts*]

Below left: This label is for POW baggage sent to the Red Cross for storage before forwarding on to his family in Germany. Since they were limited in the amount of baggage they could carry on their transport home, this service by the Red Cross filled the need for men who had acquired or created prison art or other things they wanted to keep. [*Courtesy of Gary Reeves's collection of POW artifacts*]

Below right: These POWs are returning home to Italy in January 1946 from Camp Warner, Utah (Tooele) via Oakland, CA [*Courtesy of Gary Reeves's collection of POW artifacts*].

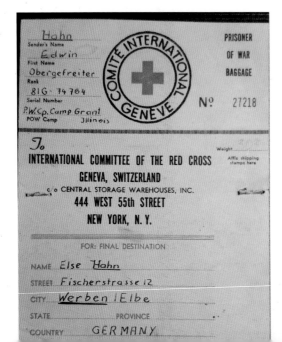

Above left: These two women have traveled from San Francisco, CA, to New York to board a U.S. military vessel to meet their former POW fiancés in Italy [*Courtesy of Gary Reeves's collection of POW artifacts*].

Above right: Of course, most of the former POWs returned to their wives and sweethearts in Italy. This is the wedding announcement for Vincenzo Lo Giudice provided by his daughter, Carmelina.

Below: This book of art was apparently created during his POW years and published later [*Courtesy of Gary Reeves's collection of POW artifacts*]

A large number of ports were utilized as departure points for the returning POWs. They included:

Los Angeles, CA
Charleston, SC
New Orleans, LA
Hampton Roads, VA
New York, NY
Boston, MA
San Francisco, CA
Seattle, WA
Halifax, Nova Scotia

Those same troop vessels were used to transport American fiancés of POWs to Naples and Genoa. These American war brides often spent a few months in Italy to complete the red tape required for a marriage there and assist their new families in rebuilding. They then brought their husbands home to America. These stories were shared by Pat and Maria Pisani and by Beth Giordana, war brides and American girls who made the trip to Italy to marry their former POW husbands.

Part of the logistics meant that after the U.S. troops returned home, their European war brides and families were shipped home on the same troop ships, slightly modified to accommodate families with small children. Be sure to see the Cary Grant movie, *I Was A Male War Bride*—it is more funny than factual, but it is based on the real transport of war brides from Europe to America.

Other former POWs made the move to live in the U.S. from ten to twenty years later. They settled in areas where they had worked as POWs, apparently in nearly every location in the country. Only local newspapers have these stories, so it is hard to get statistics. I recently found an article, "Returning to America: German Prisoners of War and the American Experience" by Barbara Schmitter Heisler (details in the bibliography).

The trip to marry in Italy was made by a young woman from Louisville, KY, who had met her husband when he was a prisoner at Camp Atterbury, Indiana. They'd met at a dance sponsored by the local Italian-American community for the Italian POWs. I met this lovely woman at a POW Reunion at Camp Atterbury in 2010 along with her children. They were regular attendees at this annual event and had wonderful stories to share. They also have a display at the Camp Atterbury Museum, across the road from the main gate to Camp Atterbury, now a reserve military training facility.

10

After the War

Some of the camps were determined to be surplus, so the property was auctioned off and the land was sold or transferred to another federal or state agency. This was a thorough process, leaving behind very little in the way of buildings to mark the former camps today.

Some of the locations had their designations changed from camp to fort. Some were originally forts, but called camps along with the rest in the PMGO records.

The POW personnel records were returned to other nations in whose military they served in 1955. The German records are now available at:

Deutsche Dienstelle (WASt)
Postfach 51 06 57
D-13400 Berlin
Germany

The Italian records are now available at:

Ministero della Difesa
via Mattia Battistini, 113, 7 Piano
00167 Roma
Italy

The Japanese records are now available at:

Military History Department National Institute for Defense Studies
2-2-1 Nakameguro, Meguro-ku
Tokyo, 153-8648
Japan

The former POWs held in the U.S. mostly held good memories of their time here. Some returned to become U.S. citizens, like Ernst Bulkat, who lived in Orem, UT. Information on them can usually be found in local papers in the 1970s and 1980s when local news groups interviewed them in a resurgence of interest in the history of the area during WWII.

The Rev. Leo Patrick worked with the POWs and persuaded some to move to Colorado after the war. The son of POW Nahomed Mueller lived with Rev. Patrick and attended Brush High School from 1950-1952.

Some former POWs returned as tourists to show their families where they'd spent part of the war. Some groups held reunions of groups of POWs who had been at a particular location to facilitate their return there with some ceremony and lots of memories. Trinidad hosted a reunion in 1964, sponsored by the town council and attended by thirteen former POWs, including Karlhorst Heil and Elert Bade, a former escapee. They held several more reunions in the 1980s and 1990s.

Some diaries and recollections have been published by former POWs. See Heino R. Erichsen's *The Reluctant Warrior: Former German POW Finds Peace in Texas* for the story of a man who later became a U.S. citizen. The grandson of one of the Italian generals, Maurizio Parri, published his grandfather's wartime diaries in *Il Giuramento; Generale a El Alamein, prigioniero in America (1942-1945)*.

Some former POWs have been gracious about allowing interviews at reunions, such as Adriano Angerilli, Enzio Luciolli, Giuseppe Margotilli, and Fernando Togni (pictured above). Some of the former, guards, prisoners and their families have become available for interviews using email, like Ernst Bulkat, Mario Iannantuoni, and August Orsini. On other occasions, I'm able to interview the children or grandchildren of a former POW in Italy or the U.S.

In 2009, one of the last reunions of former POWs visited the chapel build by POWs at Camp Hereford, TX. This is indicative of a growing awareness that these memories and relationships must be preserved through reunions, books, lectures, and movies.

Some local magazines and newspapers have done stories on the camps and published interviews with former POWs returning to visit, or who had moved back to the area where they'd been imprisoned. Some of these have been preserved by the newspaper, some by local historians, colleges, and historical societies.

A documentary, *Prisoners in Paradise*, directed by Camilla Calamandrei, tells some of the stories of several former Italian POWs.

Some local TV stations did interviews with surviving former POWs living in their communities in the 1970s and 1980s, like KUED and KSL in Salt Lake City, UT. Some local colleges (Special Collections, Stewart Library, Weber State University) created video archives containing interviews of former POWs and their families and former guards and other employees who had interaction with POWs.

Some former POWs, guards, and their families donated their diaries and photos to local historical societies, like Drew County Historical Museum in Monticello, Arkansas. Some donated to the National Archives (NARA) in College Park, Maryland. Some donated to the Stato Maggiore Esercito in Rome, Italy. I expect more will be found in local colleges and libraries in America, Italy, and Germany.

Above: This photo was taken at the 2009 reunion at Camp Hereford (TX). The U.S. Army is on the left, the former POWs center, and the Italian Air Force on the right. These men stand in front of the Chapel built by Italian POWs. [*Photo by John Saffell*]

Inset: The organization of former POWs in Italy used their old POW ID photos on their membership cards. These groups arranged reunions in Italy and at their former camps in America. Vincenzo Lo Giudice's card was provided by his daughter, Carmelina.

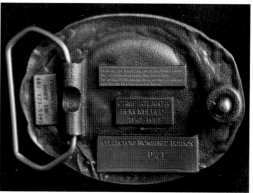

A belt buckle and lariat created for a reunion at Camp Atlanta (NE) [*Courtesy of Gary Reeves's collection of POW artifacts*]

Above left: Photo of TV interview of Joe Giordana and Gene Miconi about their POW years in Utah ASF Depot [*Courtesy of Special Collections Department, Stewart Library, Weber State University*]

Above right: This newspaper article shows the return of a former POW to Dubois, WY, to show his family where he worked as a POW [*Courtesy of the Dubois Museum*]

Former guards, like Thomas Todaro and Peter A. Pulia, Sr. also shared their memories in interviews and photos. Some, like Ralph Storm, wrote books about their experiences with POWs. Even today, I receive email from the children and grandchildren of former POWs to learn more about the experiences of being a POW in the U.S. and the hope of locating records regarding their work, health, and transfers. Most of these former POWs do not or did not talk about their experiences. Mario Turrini only told his children that Hawaii was nice, with no comment on his service in Greece, Tunisia, or his experiences at the other camps where he was held in the U.S.

Some of these letters come from Italy, but some also come from England, Australia, and the United States where these men took their families after the war.

These memories can assist us in planning for the future and promoting the preservation of photos and artifacts from the POW camps. Preservation of these memories can also be achieved by conducting interviews of surviving former POWs and their guards, and members of the community. We can use these memories and memorabilia to educate public about the policies and experiences of WWII and to promote the good treatment of future POWs.

Right: Wilson Longo (named for Woodrow Wilson) was born and died in Bellosguardo, Italy. He was a prisoner at Utah ASF Depot. His cousin, Barbara, provided this photo and information.

Below: Mary Ravarino with photos and letters from the Italian POWs from Utah ASF Depot who worked on her family's farm in Salt Lake City area. [*Photo courtesy of Italian Center of the West (UtahCulturalNews.com)*]

POW Camps by Location

There were 1,210 Prisoner of War Camps, Italian Service Unit Camps, and Prisoner of War Hospitals in the U.S.

The camp lists at NARA shows several APO addresses in place of camp names. Judging by the dates, these were located in the Philippines, Hawaii, and New Caledonia.

In Colorado, there were over 31,331 German, over 454 Italian, and 3 Japanese POWS in 51 POW camps and hospitals as follows:

Ault, Weld County, CO (branch camp under Carson). This camp opened in January 1944 and was a seasonal camp. The maximum population was 302 German POWs in June 1945, doing agricultural work. They were housed at the high school gym and attached units.

Bob's Creek, Lincoln County, CO (branch camp under Carson). This camp opened in October 1945 with its maximum population of 156 German POWs, doing agricultural work.

Brighton, Adams, and Weld Counties, CO (branch camp under Carson). This camp opened in October 1944 and was a seasonal camp. The maximum population was 589 POWs in October 1945 at the armory, old cannery, the Great Western Sugar Company cannery, and doing agricultural work.

Brush, Morgan County, CO (branch camp under Carson). This camp opened in June 1944 and was a seasonal camp. The maximum population was 501 German POWs in June 1945 doing agricultural work. They were housed at the Great Western Sugar Company terraces and dormitory and a new structure.

Carson (Camp Christopher "Kit"), near Colorado Springs, El Paso County, now Fort Carson (base camp), now an active Army installation. This camp opened in August 1943 where the POWs did military and other work (probably agricultural). The maximum population of German POWs was 8,933 in December 1945. One Italian POW is listed there also in December 1945. It had branch camps in Colorado, plus one in Sidney, Nebraska.

Center, Rio Grande and Saguache Counties, CO (branch camp under Carson). This camp opened in October 1945 with its maximum population, 220 German POWs. They were doing agricultural work and housed at the high school.

Crowley, Crowley County, CO. 300 Jamaicans and POWs lived and worked at the National Sugar Manufacturing Company facility at Bob Creek camp.

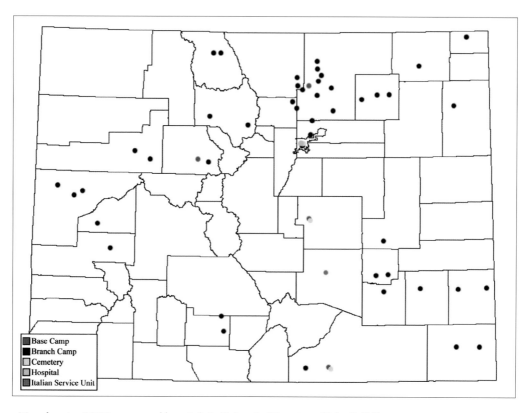

Map showing POW camps and hospitals in Colorado [*Courtesy of John Saffell*]

Deadman Mountain, Boulder County, CO (branch camp under Greeley). This camp opened in August 1944 and was a seasonal camp. The maximum population was 175 Germans in September 1945 doing forestry work.

Delta, Delta County, CO (branch camp under Carson). This camp opened in June 1945. The maximum population was 208 German POWs who lived at the Holly Sugar Corporation Camp and did agricultural work.

Eaton, Weld County, CO (branch camp under Carson). This camp opened in June 1944 and closed in November 1944. The maximum population was 210 German POWs in October 1944 doing agricultural work. They were housed at the Great Western Sugar Company dormitory.

Fitzsimmons General Hospital, Denver, Denver County, CO, was U.S. Army General Hospital; built in 1918, renamed in 1920 (sometimes a branch camp under Cook, NE). It opened as a POW camp for workers in November 1944, although it had POW patients since February 1944. The maximum POW workers were 376 Italians in April 1945. The maximum patients were 110 German POWs in July 1944, seventy-seven Italian POWs in June 1944, and three Japanese POWs in June 1944. It was renamed Fitzsimmons Army Hospital. Closed June 30, 1996 under the Defense Base Realignment and Closure Act (BRAC) of 1990. Rebuilt about 2000 as the Rocky Mountain Regional Veterans Affairs Medical Center.

Fort Collins, Larimer County, CO (branch camp under Carson). This camp opened in June 1945. The maximum population was 680 German POWs in October 1945 doing agricultural work. They were housed at the Great Western Sugar Company warehouse.

Fraser, Grand County, CO (branch camp under Greeley). This camp opened in July 1944. The maximum population was 222 German POWs in September 1945 doing agricultural and forestry work.

Fruita, Mesa County, CO (branch camp under Carson). This camp opened in June 1945. The maximum population was 275 German POWs in September 1945 doing agricultural work. They were housed at the CCC camp.

Galeton, Weld County, CO (branch camp under Carson). This camp opened in June 1945 when it achieved its maximum population of 195 German POWs doing agricultural work. They were housed at the Association extension camp.

Gilcrest, Weld County, CO (branch camp under Carson). This camp opened in October 1944 but it reached its maximum population of 126 German POWs in October 1945 doing agricultural work.

Glenwood Springs, Garfield County, CO (branch camp under Carson). This camp opened in June 1945. Its maximum population was 150 German POWs in October 1945 doing agricultural work.

Gould (Camp), Jackson County, CO (branch camp under Greeley). This camp opened in June 1944. The maximum population was 160 German POWs in October 1945 doing forestry work.

Grand Junction, Mesa County, CO (branch camp under Carson). This camp opened in September 1944 and closed in November 1944. The maximum population was 275 German POWs doing agricultural work in September 1944. They were housed in the CCC camp with Mexican nationals.

Greeley (Camp), Greeley, Weld County, CO (base camp). This camp opened in August 1943. The maximum population was 5,800 German POWs in May 1945 doing military and agricultural work. It was dismantled in 1965. The two pillars that marked the entrance were the only items to remain after auctions moved the buildings. Those pillars were moved to another location in the camp which is now part of the Cache la Poudre River National Heritage Area with signs explaining their history and stories of some of the people who were there. It had branch camps in Colorado, plus one in Ryan Park, Wyoming. Designated as Camp 202 on the National Park signage at Cache la Poudre River National Heritage Area.

Hale (Camp Irving), Pando, Eagle County, CO (branch camp under Trinidad, sometimes Carson, sometimes a base camp). This camp opened in February 1944. The maximum population was 2,870 German POWs in May 1945 doing military and other work. There was a WAC unit assigned to the hospital at this location. It was dismantled in 1965. Called Pando from November 1944.

Holly, Prowers County, CO (branch camp under Carson, later under Trinidad). This camp opened in June 1945 and reached its maximum population in November 1945 with 250 German POWs doing agricultural work. They were housed at the Holly Sugar Corporation warehouse.

Johnstown, Larimer and Weld Counties, CO (branch camp under Carson). This camp opened in October 1944 and closed in June 1945. The maximum population was 492 German POWs in June 1945 doing agricultural work. They were housed at the Great Western Sugar Company dormitory and warehouse, and at the Ford garage.

Keenesburg, Weld County, CO (branch camp under Carson). This camp opened in June 1945. The maximum population was 347 German POWs in October 1945 doing agricultural work. They were housed at the Association camp.

Kersey, Weld County, CO (branch camp under Carson). This camp opened in June 1945. The maximum population was 230 German POWs in October 1945 doing agricultural work. They were housed at the Association camp.

Kremmling, Grand County, CO (branch camp under Carson). This camp opened in February 1944 and closed in February 1945. The maximum population was 74 German POWs in December 1944 doing other work (not agricultural, forestry or military).

Lamar, Prowers County, CO (branch camp under Carson). This camp opened in October 1945 when it reached its maximum population of 132 German POWs. They were housed at the American Crystal Sugar Company hotel.

Las Animas, Bent County, CO (branch camp under Trinidad). This camp opened in October 1945 when it reached its maximum population of 119 German POWs. It was an old WFA Camp, according to the Extension Service of Colorado A&M College publication in 1947, see bibliography. Perhaps it should read WPA camp. 250 Jamaicans and POWs lived here to do agricultural work.

Logan (Fort John A.), Denver, Denver County, CO (sometimes a branch camp under Carson). The camp opened in November 1944. The maximum population was 463 German POWs in January 1945. Although the installation closed in 1946, the cemetery was retained as Fort Logan National Cemetery.

Longmont, Boulder and Weld Counties, CO (branch camp under Carson). This camp opened in June 1944 and closed in November 1944. The 415 POWs who were here lived in the Great Western Sugar Company dormitory, the County barn and County garage were doing agricultural work.

Loveland, Larimer County, CO (branch camp under Carson). This camp opened in October 1944 and closed in November 1944. The maximum population was 214 German POWs doing agricultural work. They were housed at the Great Western Sugar Company dormitory.

Minturn, Eagle County, CO (branch camp under Carson). This camp opened in July 1944 and closed in November 1944. The maximum population was 159 German POWs in August 1944 doing forestry work.

Monte Vista, Rio Grande County, CO (branch camp under Trinidad). This camp opened in February 1944. The maximum population was 558 German POWs in October 1945 doing agricultural work. They were housed at the Armory, Association camp, and the State Soldiers' Home.

Montrose, Montrose County, CO (branch camp under Carson). This camp opened in August 1945. The maximum population was 175 German POWs in October 1945. They were housed at the CCC camp.

Morgan (Fort), Morgan County, CO (branch camp under Carson). This camp opened in June 1944 and was seasonal. The maximum population was 255 German POWs in June 1945 doing agricultural work. They were housed at the Armory, store building and temporary barracks.

New Castle, Garfield County, CO (branch camp under Carson). This camp opened in August 1944 and closed in November 1944. The maximum population was 100 German POWs in September 1944 doing forestry and other work.

Ovid, Sedgwick County, CO (branch camp under Carson). This camp opened in October 1944 and was seasonal. The maximum population was 480 German POWs in October 1945 doing agricultural work. They were housed at the store building, temporary barracks, and a tent camp.

Palisade, Mesa County, CO (branch camp under Carson). This camp opened in September 1945 when it reached its maximum population of 325 German POWs. They were housed at the CCC camp.

Pando, Eagle County, CO (branch camp under Greeley, see Hale).

Pierce, Weld County, CO (branch camp under Carson). This camp opened in June 1945 when it reached its maximum population of 150 German POWs doing agricultural work. It closed that same month. They were housed in miscellaneous stores, buildings, and structures.

Pueblo Ordnance Depot, Pueblo, Pueblo County, CO (ISU, base camp) now Pueblo Chemical Weapons Storage Depot, an installation of the Army. This camp opened in September 1945 when it reached its maximum population of 212 Italian Service Unit members.

Rocky Ford, Otero County, CO (branch camp under Carson). This camp opened in June 1945. The maximum population was 174 German POWs in October 1945 doing military and agricultural work. They were housed at the fairgrounds.

Rocky Mountain Arsenal, Commerce City, Adams County, CO (branch camp under Carson). This camp opened in February 1944. The maximum population was 327 German POWs in January

1946 doing military and forestry work. Although the arsenal was closed in 1992 when it was declared the Rocky Mountain Arsenal National Wildlife Refuge, it is jointly managed by the U.S. Fish and Wildlife Service and the U.S. Army.

Springfield, Baca County, CO (branch camp under Trinidad). This location was a Civilian Conservation Corps Camp and housed 385 POWs in September and October 1945.

Sterling, Logan County, CO (branch camp under Carson, sometimes Scottsbluff, NE). This camp opened in February 1944 and was seasonal. The maximum population was 709 German POWS in October 1945 doing agricultural work. They were housed at the fairgrounds and at the Great Western Sugar Company dormitory.

Sugar City, Crowley County, CO (branch camp under Carson). This camp opened in October 1944 and was seasonal. 300 POWs lived at the fairgrounds doing agricultural work.

Trinidad (Camp), Trinidad, Las Animas County, CO (base camp). This camp opened in August 1943. The maximum population was 3,429 German POWs in February 1944 doing military and agricultural work. It had branch camps in Colorado, plus one in Elkhart, Kansas. 298 of these POWs lived at the fairgrounds.

Walden, Jackson County, CO (branch camp under Greeley). This camp opened in July 1945 and reached its maximum population of 159 German POWs in August 1945.

Walsh, Baca County, CO (branch camp under Carson). This camp opened in September 1944 and closed in November 1944. The maximum population was 315 German POWs in October 1944 doing agricultural work.

Weston (Stonewall), Las Animas County, CO (branch camp under Trinidad). This camp opened in February 1944. The maximum population was sixty-seven German POWs in March 1944 doing agricultural and forestry work.

Wiggins, Morgan County, CO (branch camp under Carson). This camp opened in June 1945. The maximum population was 350 German POWs in October 1945 doing agricultural work. They were housed at the Association camp and in tents with Jamaicans.

Yuma, Yuma County, CO (branch camp under Carson). This camp opened in November 1944. The maximum population was 150 German POWs in January 1946 doing agricultural work. They were housed at the Association camp.

12

Death Index

There were a total of 880 Germans (includes three Russians, four Austrians, one Yugoslavian, one Czech and one Turk), 172 Italians, and twenty-three Japanese (includes one Korean) out of 1,076 POWs who died while held in the U.S. during WWI & WWII. Seventeen men died or were buried in Colorado while POWs.

Baatz, Karl F.
Died and buried at Fort Logan, CO
Baehr, Ewald
Born July 12, 1927, in Bliesransbach, Saarland, Germany, died October 9, 1945, buried Camp Trinidad, CO, transferred to Fort Riley, KS
DeFalco, Antonio
Born May 29, 1918, in Napoli citta, Napoli, Italy, died July 26, 1943, and buried at Camp Trinidad, CO, transferred to Fort Riley, KS
Dietz, Alfred
Born January 9, 1922, died October 13, 1944, and buried at Camp Carson, CO, transferred to Fort Riley, KS
Frisch, Karl
Born April 9, 1921, died July 15, 1943, and buried at Camp Trinidad, CO, transferred to Fort Riley, KS. Died of gunshot wounds when shots fired at a lumber scavenging POW camp ricocheted into him.
Greco, Giacomo
Died at Fitzsimmons General Hospital, CO, buried at Camp Douglas, WY, transferred to Fort Riley, KS
Guenther, Helmut (Helmet)
Died at Fitzsimmons General Hospital, CO, buried at Camp Douglas, WY, transferred to Fort Riley, KS
Halbig, Peter
Died November 4, 1944, at Deadman Mountain, CO, buried at Fort Warren, WY
Kramer, Ernst
Born September 29, 1914, died July 26, 1943, and buried at Camp Trinidad, CO, transferred to Fort Riley, KS. Died of gunshot wounds when shots fired at a lumber scavenging POW camp ricocheted into him.

Makimo, Kazunori

Died October 29, 1944, and buried at Camp Carson, CO, transferred to Fort Riley, KS

Nachfeerg, Josef

Born August 4, 1914, died May 11, 1945, at Fitzsimmons General Hospital, CO, buried at Camp Douglas, WY, transferred to Fort Riley, KS

Nakagawa, Saburo

Died October 29, 1944, and buried at Camp Carson, CO, transferred to Fort Riley, KS

Okada, Sadamu

Died October 29, 1944, and buried at Camp Carson, CO, transferred to Fort Riley, KS

Ragozzo, Sabastiano

Died May 27, 1944, at Fitzsimmons General Hospital, CO, buried at Camp Douglas, WY, transferred to Fort Riley, KS

Schneider, Friedrich

Born July 19, 1924, died July 26, 1944, at Fitzsimmons General Hospital, CO, buried at Camp Douglas, WY, transferred to Fort Riley, KS

Schweizer, Georg

Died November 23, 1944, at Greeley, CO, buried at Fort Warren, WY

Weiner, Hugo Willi

Born April 1, 1922, died July 18, 1944, at Fitzsimmons General Hospital, CO, buried at Camp Douglas, WY, transferred to Fort Riley, KS

13

Burial Locations List

A total of 91 U.S. military and civilian cemeteries contained POW burials in the United States.

Places of Burial

Camp Carson, Colorado Springs, CO
Four WWII POW burials, transferred to Fort Riley, KS.

Camp Trinidad, CO
Four German WWII POW burials, transferred to Fort Riley, KS.

Fort Logan, Denver, CO
One German WWI POW burial still at Fort Logan National Cemetery.

Appendix A

POW Labor

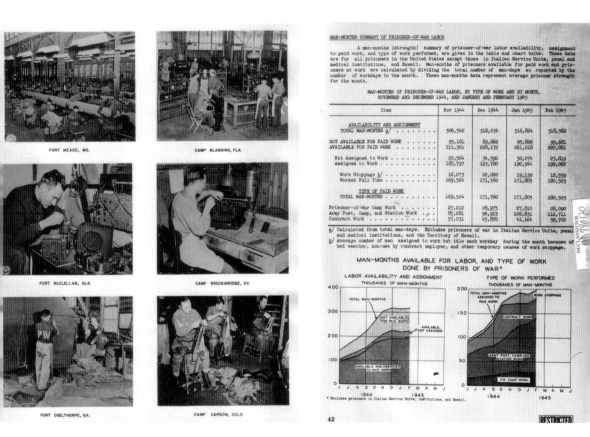

Above and next three pages: POW Work images provided by PMGO, located at NARA College Park, MD, RG 389

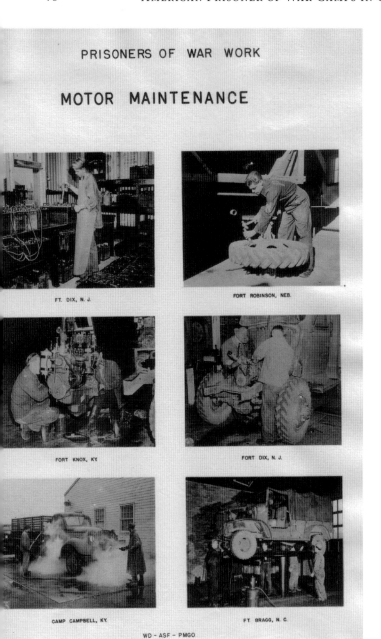

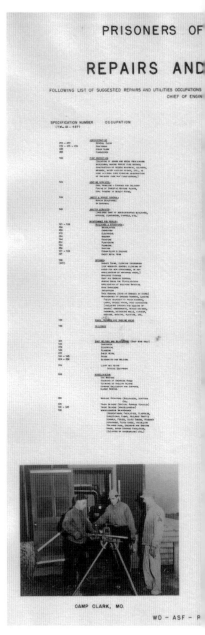

WAR WORK

UTILITIES

PRISONERS OF WAR WAS PREPARED BY OFFICE OF THE

CAMP CLARK, MO.

FORT OGELTHORPE, GA.

FORT LEONARD WOOD, MO.

TAILOR, CLOTHING REPAIR SHOP

COBBLERS, SHOE REPAIR SHOP

MECHANIC, TYPEWRITER REPAIR SHOP

OCCUPATIONS AND SKILLS OF

PRISONERS OF WAR

Auto body repairmen	Electricians
Auto painters	Auto
Auto mechanics	House
Artists	Motor
Bakers, bread and pastry	Radio
Mixers	Engravers
Oven operators	Fan cleaners
Moulders	Farm hands
Dividers	Farm machinery operato
Barbers	Firemen
Blacksmiths	Boiler and furnace
Bookkeepers	Fire department
Boot and shoe repairmen	Form builders
Boxmakers	Flashlight repairmen
Bricklayers	Freight handlers
Brushmen	Furnace cleaners
Bulldozer operators	Furnace tenders
Butchers	Furniture repairmen
Cabinetmakers	Foundry workers
Canvas workers	Garbage laborers
Carpenters	Garbage collectors
Bench	Gardners
Car	Glaziers
Concrete form	Goldsmiths
House	Graders and packers
Rough	Fruit and vegetable
Car washers and greasers	Grass mowers
Cement and concrete	Grave diggers
finishers	Greenhouse workers
Ceramic workers	Grounds keepers
Checkers	Harness makers
Chemists	Harvest hands
Sewage disposal plant	Cotton
Cleaners	Fruit
Engine	General
Floor	Sugar beets
Machine	Sugarcane
Clerks	Tobacco
General office	Vegetable
Statistical	Hospital orderlies
Stock	Incinerator operators
Clothing classifiers	Insect exterminators
Clothing repairmen	Interpreters
Coal handlers	Instrument repairmen
Cobblers	Irrigation workers
Countermen	Janitors
Concrete workers	Jewelers
Construction machinery	Kitchen police
operators	Laborer, general
Construction laborers	Language teachers
Cooks	Latrine orderlies
EM mess	Laundry workers
Officers' mess	Checker
PX restaurant	Marker
Coppersmiths	Presser
Cranemen	Sorter
Craters	Washer
Dairymen	Leather workers
Dental lab. workers	Locksmiths
Ditch diggers	Lumberyard workers
Draftsmen	Machinists
Dragline operators	Masons
Dyers	Meatcutters
Electrical repairmen	Mechanics

OCCUPATIONS AND SKILLS OF PRISONERS OF WAR (Continued)

intenance workers:
  Ditches
  Grounds
  Powerline right-of-way
  Railroad right-of-way
  Roads and streets
  Septic tanks
el and pattern makers
ders
or repairmen
  Electrical
  Gasoline and diesel
  serymen
ice-machine repairmen
kers
hopedic aide
nters
  Construction
  Maintenance
  Vehicle
er balers
otograph finishers
otographers' assistants
yaicians
ano tuners
nboys
asterers
inters
umbers
ultry dressers
apwood cutters
arry workers
dio repairmen
tion breakdown workers
pairmen
  Automobile
  Clothing
  Electrical
  Furniture
  Instrument
  Motor
  Office machine
  Radio
  Road equipment
  Shoe
  Tent
  Tire
  Typewriter
  Watch
ilroad maintenance
  workers
frigeration mechanics
ed equipment repairmen
ofers
lvage workers:
  Building materials
  Clothing and equipment
  Electrical equipment
  Motors
  Paper
e filers
wmill workers
rubmen
rvicemen, motor pool
eet metal workers

Sewage disposal plant
  operators
Shoe classifiers
Shoe repairmen
Sign painters
Silversmiths
Spray operators
  Mosquito control
  Tree spraying
Stablemen
Steam cleaners
  Vehicles
Steam fitters
Stonecutters
Stone masons
Storekeepers
Sweepers
Tailors
Teachers
Teamsters
Telephone linemen
Tent repairmen
Textile balers
Tile setters
Timekeepers
Tinsmiths
Tire changers
Tire repairmen
Tool checkers and sorters
Tool dressers and
  sharpeners
Track repairmen
Tree fallers
Tractor drivers
Truck drivers
Type setters
Typewriter repairmen
Typists
Upholsterers
  Furniture
  Vehicles
Veterinarians
Waiters
  EM mess
  Officers' club
  PX restaurant
Ward boys
Station hospital
Warehousemen
  Post ordnance
  Post quartermaster
  Salvage shop
  Post exchange
  Private industry
Wash-rock men
Watch repairmen
Water plant operators
Weavers
  Basketry
Webbing repairmen
Welders
Woodsmen
Wood workers
X-ray lab. technicians
Yardmen

MECHANICS, VEHICLE REPAIR SHOP

AUTO PAINTER, VEHICLE REPAIR SHOP

PLUMBERS, POST PLUMBING SHOP

CAMP TRINIDAD, COLO.

FORT LEONARD WOOD, MO.

CAMP SHELBY, MISS.

CAMP BRECKINRIDGE, KY.

CAMP BRECKINRIDGE, KY.

CAMP WHEELER, GA.

WD - ASF - PMGO

POST ENGINEER WORK

CAMP CLINTON, MISS.

EDGEWOOD ARSENAL, MD.

GALVESTON AAB, TEX.

CAMP SUTTON, N. C.

CAMP CARSON, COLO.

FORT LEONARD WOOD, MO.

POST ENGINEER WORK

FORT BENJAMIN HARRISON, IND.

NORFOLK ARMY AIR BASE, VA.

CAMP BRECKINRIDGE, KY.

CAMP CLINTON, MISS.

INSTRUCTIONS TO THE CONTRACTOR
UNDER CONTRACT FOR PRISONER OF WAR LABOR

The treatment and employment of prisoners of war are governed by an international treaty called the Geneva Convention. The United States Government is bound to follow the terms of this treaty. It is also important to do so, and to treat enemy prisoners fairly, in order to avoid appraisals against American Prisoners held by enemy countries. As a contractor using prisoner of war labor you have agreed and are required to obey the provisions of the Geneva Convention. You have also agreed and are required to comply with War Department security regulations relative to prisoners of war. The following instructions have been prepared for your guidance:

1 In case of any escape or unwarranted conduct on the part of any prisoner of war, you should inform the guard detail commander in charge of the prisoners, who is responsible for their conduct. You should make your telephone available to him so that he may phone the camp commander at any time.

2 You should not fraternize with prisoners of war or allow third persons to do so. If you fraternize with them, and there is an escape, your action might tend to make it appear you had helped in the escape. Helping a prisoner of war to escape is a serious criminal offense.

3 In addition to precautions taken by the guards, you should exercise every reasonable care that prisoners do not escape from your premises. You should cooperate fully with the military authorities and guards in the matter of taking steps to avoid escapes.

4 You should not allow prisoners to wear clothing other than that issued by the War Department. Their clothing has been marked to identify them as prisoners of war. Do not give them old hats or coats to wear.

5 You should fully occupy the time of the prisoners. If a situation arises where they cannot work, notify the guard detail commander so the prisoners can be returned to camp instead of being idle around your premises.

6 All prisoner of war mail, even to persons in the United States, must be censored. Therefore it is very important that you cooperate fully with the guard detail commander in preventing any prisoner from mailing letters, cards, packages or cards from your premises, and in preventing third persons who might smuggle mail from mixing with the prisoners. Prisoners must not make telephone calls or send cables or telegrams. You should report to the guard detail commander any violations of this rule.

7 The guard detail commander is responsible that only authorized newspaper reporters, news photographers or newsreel cameramen attempt to secure information or photographs the prisoners of war. You must cooperate with the guard in this respect. You yourself should not give out any publicity regarding the prisoners of war.

8 You do not need workmen's compensation insurance for the benefit of the prisoners of war performing work under your contract. This matter is covered by War Department regulations.

9 Your civilian employees and others who may come in contact with the prisoners of war in the performance of the contract should be informed of these instruction and should be enjoined to carry them out.

10 The War Department expects your cooperation in these matters so that the prisoner of war labor program will be successful. Failure on your part to follow these instructions, and other instructions given you by the military authorities, may result in cancellation of the contract and refusal of the War Department to furnish prisoner of war labor to you in the future.

11 The Government reserves the right to supplement or change these instructions. These instructions do not in any way modify or limit your obligations under the contract.

12 This bulletin should be posted in such places in or around your establishment so that these instructions may be known to all civilian personnel employed by you.

SUPPLEMENT "A"

1a. It is your responsibility to furnish all supervision necessary for the efficient operation of any prisoner of war detail. Guards are responsible for the safe guarding of prisoners of war and should not be expected to direct prisoner of war labor for the contractor.

2a. You should refrain from taking any disciplinary action regarding prisoners of war, as no prisoner of war can be forced to work. Need for any disciplinary action should be reported to the guard, and his instructions should be followed.

3a. Always remember that the way you treat prisoners of war determines the treatment given American soldiers who are prisoners of war in German hands.

Hq. 1663rd SU Form No. 33

Above: POW contract instructions [*Courtesy of Gary Reeves's collection of POW artifacts*]

Below: POW labor in Sixth Service Command [*Courtesy of Gary Reeves's collection of POW artifacts*]

RESTRICTED

ARMY SERVICE FORCES
HEADQUARTERS, SIXTH SERVICE COMMAND
Chicago 6, Illinois

6 May 1944

In Reply Refer To: SPJIP 383.6

To: All Law Enforcement Agencies,
     States of Illinois, Michigan, and Wisconsin

During the coming summer months, it is contemplated to have German prisoners of war working on various agricultural projects in the States of Illinois, Michigan, and Wisconsin, and it is with the thought of a possible escape from one of these projects, that the following is given for your official information and not general publication:

I. Prisoners of war are in the custody of the War Department and their treatment as prisoners of war is covered by the Geneva Convention of 1929. Germany and the United States are both subscribers to this Convention and the treatment that is accorded German prisoners of war in this country is reflected in the treatment accorded Americans held as prisoners of war by the German Government. The Geneva Convention is reproduced by the Government Printing Office, Washington, D.C., and can be obtained for a nominal fee.

II. Prisoners of war are not prisoners in the commonly accepted usage of that term by law enforcement officers. Neither are they fugitives from justice. Unless, in an escapee status, they violate some civil law of the United States, State or municipality, they should be treated as honorable soldiers. Prisoners of war, unless guilty of some civil offense, should not be handcuffed or placed in common cells. If apprehended by civil authorities, they should be restrained under guard until they can be turned over to the nearest military authorities. Experience develops that German prisoners will be found to be amenable to authority and very unlikely to offer any resistance to arrest.

III. Prisoners of war have a legal right to attempt to escape and it may be assumed at all times that they will endeavor to attempt to escape if the opportunity presents itself. As members of the armed forces of the enemy, they may be expected to have a constant, fixed intention to advance as much as possible the aims and aspirations of their country. They may also be expected to attempt to communicate with enemy sympathizers, to acquire and transmit information of military value or to cause damage, delay, or other acts to deter our war effort.

IV. (A) Articles of the U.S. Army uniform are not issued unless altered in a manner that will prevent them from being mistaken for parts of the Army uniform, such as, removing all official buttons on all undyed articles of the U.S. Army uniform, and replacing them with buttons, bone or

SPJIP 383.6, 6 May 1944 (Continued)

VI. Your cooperation in giving assistance when requests are made by representatives of the War Department, in connection with the operation of prisoner of war "Labor Details", will be appreciated.

W. E. GUTHRIE
Brigadier General, G.S.C.
Director
Security and Intelligence Division

WAR DEPARTMENT

CONTRACT FOR LABOR OF PRISONERS OF WAR

PRISONER OF WAR CAMP:

Contract No. W ___03-044-___ pmg _76_

___Monticello, Arkansas___

[This contract is authorized by and has been negotiated under the First War Powers Act, 1941, and Executive Order No. 9001]

THIS CONTRACT, entered into this ___19th___ day of ___June 1945___, between the

UNITED STATES OF AMERICA

hereinafter referred to as the Government, represented by the contracting officer executing this contract and ___Ozark Badger Lumber Company___

(*) ___A corporation organized under the laws of Arkansas___

whose address is ___Wilmar, Arkansas___

hereinafter called the contractor, WITNESSETH, that the parties mutually agree as follows:

1. LABOR.—The Government will furnish the Contractor the labor of prisoners of war in the following amount:
   (a) Number of men each work day ___16___
   (b) Number of work days ___78___
   (c) Labor will be furnished commencing on or about ___20 June 1945___ and ending on or about ___20 Sept. 45.___
   (d) Normal work day will consist of ___10___ hours of labor (*Excluding lunch and travel time*).
   (e) The address of the work site is ___Vicinity of Wilmar, Arkansas___
   (f) Type of work is ___Cutting of Pine Timber (Faller)___

2. TRANSPORTATION, TOOLS, ETC.
   (a) Transportation for prisoners of war and guards from the camp to the work site and return to the camp will be furnished by the ___Contractor___
   (b) Distance between camp and work site is ___13___ miles.
   (c) Tools and equipment will be furnished by the ___Contractor___
   (d) Maintenance of tools and equipment will be provided by the ___Contractor___
   (e) Other items ___None___

3. COMPENSATION.—The Contractor will pay to the Government compensation at the following rates:
   (a) Labor ___$2.50 per 1000 ft. 16 prisoners cutting 32,000 ft. = $80.00 per day___
   ___$80.00 x 78 days = $6,240.00___

   (b) Transportation ___Furnished by Contractor at his expense___

   (c) Other items ___None___

4. ALLOWANCES.—The Government will grant the Contractor allowances as follows:
   (a) Transportation ___None___

   (b) Other items ___None___

5. VALUE OF CONTRACT (*Estimated*)
   Gross charges $ ___6,240.00___   Allowances $ ___None___   Net charges $ ___6,240.00___

6. If the Contractor fails to utilize fully the labor of prisoners of war in accordance with paragraph 1, above, the loss and damage to the Government resulting from the reduction in essential war production for which such labor could have been utilized will be impossible to determine, and in place thereof, the Contractor shall pay to the Government the sum of $1.50 per day for each prisoner whose labor is not so utilized, unless the failure to utilize such labor was due to unusually severe weather, acts of God, or other unforeseeable causes clearly beyond the control of the Contractor.

7. As a condition to the execution of this contract, the Contractor has furnished security for payment to the War Department in the form of (†) CASH DEPOSIT—BANK GUARANTEE—SURETY BOND, to guarantee the satisfactory settlement of accounts due for labor furnished under the provisions of this contract. The total security for payment required for this contract is $ ___6,240.00___ of which $ ___None___ is represented by the Contractor's investment in branch camp construction, and $ ___6,240.00___ is in the form indicated above, satisfactory evidence of which is attached hereto. (*Certificate of surety, bank guarantee, or escrow agreement for cash deposits.*)

8. The Government will furnish meals for prisoners and guards unless otherwise provided in this contract.

9. The Contractor agrees to furnish adequate training instruction and work supervision.

10. The Contractor will not be responsible for disability compensation or medical care for the prisoners of war.

11. The Contractor agrees to make payment to the Contracting Officer, by certified or cashier's check, or United States Post Office money order, payable to the Treasurer of the United States, within 10 days after receipt of bill or invoice.

(*) Describe as: "An individual trading as * * *"; "A partnership consisting of * * *"; or, "A corporation organized under the laws of the State of * * *."
(†) Strike out types of security for payment not applicable.

16-44345-1

WD AGO FORM 19-19
1 MAY 1945

Above and next three pages: Work contracts for civilians to obtain POW labor [*Courtesy of Michael Pomeroy*]

-2-

2. Conditions of employment offered by this employer are not less favorable than those for other workers in the same or similar employment at this establishment or farm, or less favorable than those prevailing in the locality for similar work.

3. The prevailing wage, or price per unit, certified above is that paid to free labor in this locality for this type of work. (For agricultural work, the prevailing wage, or price per unit, certified by the State Director of Extension may be based on public hearings conducted by County Farm Wage Boards.)

4. It has been impossible to secure the necessary workers for this employer through an active campaign of recruitment which has taken into account not only all persons normally engaged in the activities listed above, but also potential workers from other fields of activities.

5. The employer is willing to use through contract with the Government, the labor of prisoners of war detained by the United States of America and in the custody of the War Department. It is the understanding of the undersigned that such contract will follow substantially War Department contract form for prisoners of war and that amount to be paid and conditions stated in the contract will be in accord with those certified in this statement.

INDORSEMENTS

1. Approval of the above certificate is recommended:

Louise C. Thompson   Manager
(signature)   (title)

6-19-1945   308 North Main St. Monticello, Arkansas
(date)   (address)

II. The above certificate is approved:

Ward Dunn   Deputy Regional Director
(signature)   (title)

6-23-45   1600 Fidelity Bldg., Kansas City 6, Mo.
(date)   (address)

III. The labor certified above has been determined to fall in priority   2

Denton O. Rushing   State Manpower Director
(signature)   (title)

5-21-45   Old Post Office Bldg., Little Rock, Arkansas
(date)   (address)

CERTIFICATION OF NEED FOR EMPLOYMENT
OF PRISONERS OF WAR

To: Commanding General,
___8th___ Service Command

Attention: ___Commanding Officer, Monticello Prisoner of War Camp___

The ___War Manpower Commission___ certifies that:

1. The employer to whom this certificate is issued and whose name, address and place of business are listed below, has need for the labor hereinafter described for essential work at his establishment or farm.

a. Name of employer ___Ozark Badger Lumber Company___

b. Address of employer ___Wilmar, Arkansas___

c. Type of business ___cutting of pine timber___

d. Location of work (if not at above address) ___vicinity of Wilmar, Arkansas___

e. Labor needed: From ___6-20-1945___ to ___9-20-1945___
       (date)   (date)
   For period of approximately ___3 months___   ~~days~~-months
                                 (number)   (cross out one)

f. Detail of type of work, number of prisoners, and wage rates:

Number needed	Occ. Title and Code for Industry or Nature of Work Done for Agric.	Man Days or Hours Required	Unit of Work	Prevailing wage per unit
16	Faller — 6-30.140 (cutting pine logs)	416 man days per mo.	by 1000 ft.	$2.50 per 1000 ft.

These prisoners are to be used only at such times as soil and weather conditions prevent their use in agriculture

g. If at piece rate, average
   civilian labor will complete ___2 to 3___ units per day.
                                  (number)

h. The employer usually furnished the following services free of charge to civilian labor: *
   ___tools - transportation___

i. The employer ___will___ supply transportation to and from the
              (will or will not)
   prisoner-of-war enclosure.

j. The employer ___will not___ provide the noonday meal.
              (will or will not)

k. Length of work day in this locality
   for this type of work is customarily ___8___ hours.
                                       (number)

* Enter, if appropriate, one or more of the following: transportation to and from work; noon meal; housing accommodations.

12. The Contractor agrees to maintain conditions of employment in conformity with War Department regulations applicable to the employment of prisoners of war on the type of work described in this contract. The Contractor will comply with all written directions of the Government for the correction or improvement of conditions of employment found by the Government to be in violation of the Geneva Convention and for security and safety measures. The Contractor acknowledges the receipt of an "Instructions to the Contractor for Prisoner-of-War Labor" and agrees to observe these instructions and any amendments or additions that the Government may make in such instructions.

13. The Contractor agrees that duly accredited representatives of the Government and the protecting power will at all times have access to the site of the work in order to observe the conditions of employment.

14. The Contractor agrees that he has no authority to impose disciplinary measures on prisoners of war.

15. The Contractor agrees to permit the Government to maintain at the site of the work such guards and other security measures as may be found by the Government to be desirable or necessary, and to cooperate fully with the Government in all security measures.

16. If it be found by the Government that the Contractor has suffered damages to his property or to property for which he is responsible to a third party, uncompensated by insurance, arising out of the employment of prisoners of war, and not the result of fault or negligence of the Contractor, which are caused by the willful misconduct of prisoners, the Government (*without prejudice to any other rights which the Contractor may have*) will allow the amount of such damages as a credit against payments otherwise due from the Contractor hereunder; but no such credit shall be taken without the specific approval of the Government, nor shall the liability of the Government under this paragraph for any such damages exceed the unpaid amounts due from the Contractor at the time he files a claim for property damage and from amounts which subsequently become due under the terms of this contract.

17. This contract may be terminated by either party, with or without cause, by 10 days' notice in writing. In event of termination the Contractor will pay to the Government, at the rates herein set forth, all charges accrued up to the effective date of termination.

18. No member of or delegate to Congress or resident commissioner shall be admitted to any share or part of this contract or to any benefit that may arise therefrom, but this provision shall not be construed to extend to this contract if made with a corporation for its general benefit.

19. The Contractor warrants that he has not employed any person to solicit or secure this contract upon any agreement for a commission, percentage, brokerage, or contingent fee. Breach of this warranty shall give the Government the right to annul the contract, or at its option, to recover from the Contractor the amount of such commission, percentage, brokerage, or contingent fee, in addition to the consideration herein set forth. This warranty shall not apply to commissions payable by the Contractor upon contracts secured or made through bona fide established commercial agencies maintained by the Contractor for the purpose of doing business.

20. Except as otherwise specifically provided in this contract, all disputes concerning questions of fact which may arise under this contract, and which are not disposed of by mutual agreement, shall be decided by the Contracting Officer, who shall reduce his decision to writing and mail a copy thereof to the Contractor. Within 30 days from said mailing the Contractor may appeal to the Secretary of War, whose decision or that of his designated representative, representatives, or board shall be final and conclusive upon the parties hereto. Pending decision of a dispute hereunder the Contractor shall diligently proceed with the performance of this contract.

21. Except for the original signing of this contract, the term "Contracting Officer" as used herein shall include his duly appointed successor or his authorized representative.

22. The "Certification of Need for Employment of Prisoners of War" attached to this contract is for the information and guidance of the appropriate contracting parties and is not a part of this contract.

23. The following changes were made, and addenda attached, to this contract before it was signed by the parties hereto:

Payment to the Contracting Officer by certified or cashier's check or U. S. money order payable to the Treasurer of the United States will be made by the Contractor on or about the tenth of each month for labor furnished during the preceding month.

IN WITNESS WHEREOF, the parties hereto have executed this contract on the day and year first above written.

Witness:

Doris H. Strachan

Monticello, Ark (Address)

Witness:

Elizabeth W. Chandler

Monticello, Arkansas (Address)

THE UNITED STATES OF AMERICA:

By *Jas. H. Kutner*

JAMES H. KUTNER
Colonel, Infantry

Contracting Officer.

Contractor:

OZARK-BADGER LUMBER COMPANY

By *L. K. Pomeroy*

L. K. POMEROY, President

I, *E. P. Connor*, certify that I am the Assistant Secretary of the Corporation named as Contractor herein; that *L. K. Pomeroy* who signed this contract on behalf of the Contractor was then *President* of said Corporation; that said contract was duly signed for and on behalf of said Corporation by authority of its governing body and is within the scope of its corporate powers.

IN WITNESS WHEREOF, I have hereunto affixed my hand and the seal of said corporation this ____16____ day of ____July____, 1945.

E. P. Connor

Assistant Secretary.

U. S. GOVERNMENT PRINTING OFFICE   16—44345-1

Appendix B

Museums and Websites

Arizona Historical Society Museum, Papago Park, AZ - www.arizonahistoricalsociety.org/museums

Billion Graves – www.billiongraves.com

Cache la Poudre River National Heritage Area - https://poudreheritage.org/locations/wwii-pow-camp-202/

Camp Aliceville - www.encyclopediaofalabama.org/face/Article.isp?id-2322

Camp Hearne Museum – camphearne.com/index.htm

Camp Opelika – www.eastalabama.org/Exhibits/Exhibits.htm

Camp Ruston – www.latech.edu/library/scma/index.php

Camp Van Dorn World War II Museum – www.vandorn.org

Camp White Military Museum located in the VA SORCC facility in White City, OR

Cemetery Records Online - www.interment.net

Door County Maritime Museum, Sturgeon Bay, WI, has display on WWII POWs in the area orchards.

Drew County Museum, Monticello, AR, has a display on WWII POWs at Camp Monticello.

Family Search - familysearch.org

Find a Grave - www.findagrave.com

Fort Douglas, Salt Lake City, UT – www.fortdouglas.org/about/virtual-tour, also cemetery

Fort George G. Meade Museum - www.ftmeade.army.mil/museum/Museum_POW.html

Fort Leonard Wood Museum - www.visitmo.com/museums-at-fort-leonard- wood.aspx

GenTracer – World War II - www.gentracer.org

German War Graves Commission – www.volksbund.de

Greeley History Museum - 714 8th Street, Greeley, CO 80631, Phone: (970) 351-9219, Email: museums@greeleygov. com, URL: http://greeleymuseums.com/

Library of Congress – catalog.loc.gov

March Field Air Museum, Riverside, CA - www.marchfield.org

Mississippi Armed Forces Museum, Camp Shelby, MS - www.armedforcesmuseum.us/Pages/Newsletter.pdf

Mountain Empire Historical Society and Stone Museum, Campo, CA at www.cssmus.org/

Traces – www.traces.org

Tracy Historical Museum, 1141 Adams St., Tracy, CA

Trinidad History Museum, 312 E. Main St., Trinidad, CO

U.K. National Archives - www.nationalarchives.gov.uk

U.S. Dept. of Veterans Affairs National Cemeteries at www.cem.va.gov/cem/cems/listcem.asp

U.S. National Archives and Records Administration – www.archives.gov

U. S. National Park Service - www.nps.gov

Weber State University, Stewart Library, Special Collections Exhibits, "Prisoners of War in Ogden" at library.weber. edu/collections/special_collections

Bibliography

Adams, Meredith Lentz. "A Miscarriage of Justice?" interview by Jim Kelly. Sunflower Journeys Home 16101A. KTWU. 2003.

_____. *Murder and Martial Justice: Spying and Retribution in World War II America*. Kent, Ohio: Kent State University Press, 2011.

_____. "The Abortive Attempt to Exchange GI and German POWs". (Presentation, TRACES conference, 31 May 2003).

Amdt, Karl John Richard. "German P.O.W. Camp Papers." Microfilm. Washington, DC: Library of Congress Photo-duplication Service, 1965. Library of Congress. lccn.loc.gov/83125121.

Angerilli, Adriano. Interview by author. 14 August 2009.

Army Service Forces. "Service Command Operating Personnel and Prisoners, 31 March 1945", NARA RG 389, Entry 261, Box 2563. National Archives at College Park, College Park, MD.

Bland, John Paul. *Secret War at Home: The Pine Grove Furnace Prisoner of War Interrogation Camp*. Cumberland County Historical Society, Carlisle, PA, 2006.

Boni, Andrea. Interview by author. 3 November 2018.

Boudreaux, Henry J, Capt., C.M.P. Report of Investigation of the deaths of Leonello Bini, Vito Clemente, Adolfo Nitri, Antonino Paleologo, 21 July 1943, NARA RG 389, Entry 461, Box 2562. National Archives at College Park, College Park, MD.

Bryan, B.M., Brigadeer General. Assistant Provost Marshal General, Letter to Army Services Forces regarding transfer of POWs, 26 August 1944, NARA RG 389, Entry 457, Box 1419. National Archives at College Park, College Park, MD.

Bulkat, Ernst. Interview by author. 11 March 2007.

Bykofsky, *Joseph and Harold Larson. United States Army in World War II: The Technical Services: The Transportation Corps: Operations Overseas*. Center of Military History, United States Army, Washington, DC, 2003.

Carlson, Lewis. "POW Experience: Myth and Reality." (Presentation, TRACES conference, 6 October 2002).

Conn, Stetson and Byron Fairchild. *The United States Army in World War II, The Western Hemisphere, The Framework of Hemisphere Defense*. Washington, DC: Office of the Chief of Military History, Department of the Army, 1960.

Conn, Stetson and Rose C Engelman and Byron Fairchild, *The United States Army in World War II, The Western Hemisphere, Guarding the United States and its Outposts*. Washington, DC: Office of the Chief of Military History, Department of the Army, 1964

Corbin, Alexander, *The History of Camp Tracy: Japanese WWII POWs and the Future of Strategic Interrogation*. Fort Belvoir, VA: Ziedon Press, 2009

Cosentini, George and Norman Gruenzner. *United States Numbered Military Post Offices Assignments and Locations 1941-1994*. The Military Postal History Society, 1994.

Cowley, Betty. *Stalag Wisconsin: Inside WWII Prisoner-of-war Camps*. Oregon, WI: Badger Books, 2002.

Cunningham, Raymond Kelly. *Prisoners at Fort Douglas: War Prison Barracks Three and the alien enemies, 1917-1920.* Salt Lake City, UT: Fort Douglas Military Museum, 1983.

Daugherty, Joseph B., Col. Assistant, Office of the Quartermaster General, Letter to Provost Marshal General regarding repatriation of ISU units, dated 9 October 1945, NARA RG 389, Entry 261, Box 2563. National Archives and Records Administration, College Park, MD

_____. Letter to Provost Marshal General regarding repatriation of ISU units, dated 28 August 1945, NARA RG 389, Entry 261, Box 2563. National Archives and Records Administration, College Park, MD

"Department of Veterans Affairs National Cemeteries," United States Department of Veterans Affairs, www.cem.va.gov/cem/cems/listcem.asp.

Ducharme, Joseph O.C., Lt. Col. Director, Enemy PW Information Bureau, Camp Holabird, MD, to Provost Marshal General, regarding cemetery locations, dated 16 February 1953, NARA RG 389, Entry 261, Box 2562. National Archives and Records Administration, College Park, MD

_____. Regarding cemetery locations, dated 16 February. 1953, NARA RG 389, Entry 467, Box 1513. National Archives and Records Administration, College Park, MD

Dvorak, Petula. "Fort Hunt's Quiet Men Break Silence on WWII: Interrogator Fought "Battle of Wits."" The Washington Post. 6 October 2007.

Edwards, Earl L., Lt. Col. Asst. Dir., Prisoner of War Division, Letter to Army Services Forces, regarding prisoner segregation, dated 3 March 1944, NARA RG 389, Entry 261, Box 2563. National Archives and Records Administration, College Park, MD

_____. Letter Regarding Prisoner Transfer, dated 16 October 1943, NARA RG 389, Entry 261, Box 2563. National Archives and Records Administration, College Park, MD

_____. Letter Regarding Prisoner Transfer, dated 7 January 1943, NARA RG 389, Entry 261, Box 2563. National Archives and Records Administration, College Park, MD

Enemy Prisoner of War Information Bureau. "World War II Enemy Prisoners of War Deceased in Theaters of Operations, Fort Holabird, MD, 2 July 1952", NARA RG 389, Entry 466, Box 1. National Archives and Records Administration, College Park, MD

Eppinga, Jane. *Death at Papago Park POW Camp: A Tragic Murder and America's Last Mass Execution.* Charleston, SC: The History Press, 2017.

Erichsen, Heino R. *The Reluctant Warrior: Former German POW Finds Peace in Texas.* Austin, TX: Eakin Press, 2001.

_____. Interview by author. 7 October 2002.

Extension Service (Anderson, F.A.), "A Resume of the Emergency Farm Labor Program in Colorado (1943-1947 Inclusive)". Colorado A&M College, Fort Collins, CO, 1947.

Fairchild, Byron and Jonathan Grossman. *United States Army in World War II: The War Department: The Army and Industrial Manpower.* Center of Military History, Department of the Army, Washington, DC, 2002.

Farrand, Stephen M. Major, Prisoner of War Operations Division, Letter to Special War Problems Division regarding the death of Karl Schaeffer, dated 28 May 1945, NARA RG 389, Entry 261, Box 2562. National Archives and Records Administration, College Park, MD

_____. Letter to Special War Problems Division regarding the death of Alfred Malinowski, dated 20 February 1945, NARA RG 389, Entry 261, Box 2562. National Archives and Records Administration, College Park, MD

"Find a Grave," Find a Grave, www.findagrave.com.

Fischer, H. P., Office of the Commanding General, Ninth Service Command, Fort Douglas, UT, Letter to Army Service Forces regarding new base camps, dated 31 March 1945, NARA RG 389, Entry 457, Box 1419. National Archives and Records Administration, College Park, MD

Ford, George. "German Guard Held in Medical Ward After Shooting 28 Germans: Probe Opened by Army Into Salina Affair". The Deseret News, 9 July 1945.

Frank, Dave & David E. Seelye. *The Complete Book of World War II U.S.A POW & Internment Camp Chits: Prisoner of War Money in the United States.* Coin and Currency Institute, Williston, VT, 2019

Gansberg, Judith M., Stalag: *U.S.A: The Remarkable Story of German POWs in America.* New York, NY: Thomas Y. Crowell Company, 1977.

German War Graves Commission at www.volksbund.de

Giordana, Beth. Interview by author. August 2001.

Griffith, L.E. Lt. Col., Prisoner of War Operations Division, Letter to Mrs. Ada Errera regarding transfer of body to Italy, dated 30 April 1946, NARA RG 389, Entry 261, Box 2562. National Archives and Records Administration, College Park, MD

Hamann, Jack. *On American Soil: How Justice Became a Casualty of World War II.* Algonquin Books, 2005.

Hanson, Tor. *Images of America: Camp Abbot.* Arcadia Publishing, 2018

Heisler, Barbara Schmitter. "Returning to America: German Prisoners of War and the American Experience", *German Studies Review,* Vol. 31, No. 3 (Oct., 2008), pp. 537-556; Published by: Johns Hopkins University Press on behalf of the German Studies Association

Heitmann, John A. "Enemies are Human." (Presentation, Dayton Christian-Jewish Dialogue, 10 May 1998).

Iannantuoni, Mario. Interview by author. 10 February 2012.

Janet Worrall POW Camp 202 Collection. Hazel E Johnson Research Center, Greeley History Museum. http://greeleymuseums.com/

Jensen, Carol A. *Images of America: Byron Hot Springs.* San Francisco, CA: Arcadia Publishing, 2006.

Jepson, Daniel A. "Historical and Archaeological Perspectives on the World War II Prisoner of War Camp at Fort Carson, Colorado", Centennial Archaeology, Inc. Fort Collins, CO. 1990.

Jones, L.B.C. Lt. Col. Deputy Director, Internal Security Division, Regarding Security, dated 14 October 1943, NARA RG 389, Entry 261, Box 2563. National Archives and Records Administration, College Park, MD

Keefer, Louis E., *Italian Prisoners of War in America, 1942-1946: Captives or Allies?* New York, NY: Praeger, 1992.

Kirkpatrick, Kathy. "Italian POWs in Utah." (Presentation, TRACES conference, 7 October 2002)

_____ (Presentation, TRACES conference 31 May 2003).

Kleinman, Steven M. "The History of MIS-Y: U.S. Strategic Interrogation During World War II". Master's thesis, Joint Military Intelligence College, 2002.

Knappe, Siegfried & Ted Brusaw. *Soldat: Reflections of a German Soldier 1936-1949.* New York, NY: Orion Books, 1992.

Krammer, Arnold. "American Treatment of German Generals" *The Journal of Military History* 54, No. 1 (January 1990): 27-46.

_____. "German Prisoners of War in the United States" *Military Affairs* 40, No. 2 (April 1976): 68-73.

_____. *Nazi Prisoners of War in America.* Lanham, MD: Scarborough House, 1996.

Landsberger, Kurt, *Prisoners of War at Camp Trinidad, Colorado 1943-1946: Internment, Intimidation, Incompetence and Country Club Living.* Arbor Books, 2007.

Leighton, Richard M., and Robert W. Coakley. *The United States Army in World War II, The War Department, Global Logistics and Strategy 1940-1943,* Washington, DC: Office of the Chief of Military History, Department of the Army, 1955.

Lewis, George G, and John Mewha. *History of Prisoner of War Utilization by the United States Army, 1776-1945.* U.S. Department of the Army, Pamphlet 20-213, Washington, DC: Government Printing Office, 1955.

Listman, John, Christopher Baker, and Susan Goodfellow. Historic Context: World War II Prisoner-of-war Camps on Department of Defense Installations. Department of Defense Legacy Resource Management Program, 10 July 2007.

L'Ufficio Informazione Vaticano per I pregionieri di guerra istituito da Pio XII, Vatican Secret Archives. Vatican City.

Lucioli, Ezio. Interview by author. 14 August 2009.

Luick-Thrams, Michael. "The Fritz Ritz: German POWs in the American Heartland" (Presentation, TRACES conference, 31 May 2003).

Margotilli, Giuseppe. Interview by author. 14 August 2009.

Martin, Charles E., Col., Director of Personnel, Memorandum to Armed Service Forces, regarding release of ISU, dated 3 October 1945, NARA RG 389, Entry 261, Box 2563. National Archives and Records Administration, College Park, MD

_____. Memorandum to Armed Service Forces, regarding release of ISU, dated 23 August 1945, NARA RG 389, Entry 261, Box 2563. National Archives and Records Administration, College Park, MD

_____. Memorandum to Armed Service Forces, regarding release of ISU, dated 20 August 1945, NARA RG 389, Entry 261, Box 2563. National Archives and Records Administration, College Park, MD

Mills, James E. "A History of Brush, Colorado." Master's Thesis, University of Colorado, 1965.

Moore, John Hammond. "Italian POWs in America: War is Not Always Hell." Prologue (Fall 1976): 141-151.

_____. *Wacko War: Strange Tales from America 1941-1945*. Raleigh, NC: Pentland Press, 2001.

Muller, Eric L. "Betrayal on Trial: Japanese-American 'Treason' in World War II." North Carolina Law Review 82.5, June 2004.

Nagler, Joerg A. "Enemy Aliens and Internment in World War I: Alvo von Alvensleben in Fort Douglas, Utah, a Case Study." *Utah Historical Quarterly* 58 (Fall 1990): 388-406

Nash, Gerald D. *The American West Transformed: The Impact of the Second World War*. Bloomington, IN: Indiana University Press, 1985.

National Archives and Records Administration, Record Group 38. Records of the Navy; Special Activities Branch (OP-16-Z), Navy Unit, Tracy, California. National Archives and Records Administration, College Park, MD

_____. Record Group 331. Records of Allied Operational and Occupation Headquarters, World War II. Entry 3A, Box 126. Repatriation to USSR National Archives and Records Administration, College Park, MD

_____. Record Group 389. Records of the Office of the Provost Marshal General. National Archives and Records Administration, College Park, MD

Nisei Sisters, https://coloradoencyclopedia.org/article/nisei-sisters

O'Neill, Caroline. "Pueblo Chemical Depot" in Colorado Encyclopedia at coloradoencyclopedia.org/article/pueblo-chemical-depot.

Orsini, August. Interview by author. 7 October 2011.

Palermo, Raffaele. "ISU Personnel Records." Al Ministero della Difesa, Rome, Italy.

Parri, Dino. *Il Giuramento; Generale a El Alamein, prigioniero in America (1942-1945)*. Milano: Mursia, 2009.

Paschal, Allen W. "The Enemy in Colorado: German Prisoners of War, 1943-1946", *Colorado Magazine*. Summer-Fall 1979.

"Per il Soldato Francesco Erriquez la guerra è finita!," Un Mondo di Italiani, www.unmondoditaliani.com/per-il-soldato-francesco-erriquez-la-guerra-e-finita.htm.

Pisani, Pat and Maria. Interview by author. 12 June 2009.

Powell, Allan Kent. *Splinters of a Nation; German Prisoners of War in Utah*. Salt Lake City, UT: University of Utah Press, 1989.

Prendergast, Alan. For Nazi Officers, Trinidad's POW Camp

Was the Great Escape, https://www.westword.com/content/printView/9679327

Prisoners in Paradise, DVD, directed by Camilla Calamandrei. 2001.

"Prisoners of War in Ogden: 1943-1946," Weber State University Stewart Library, ibrary.weber.edu/asc/POW/default.cfm.

Prosecution of the Shitara Sisters, Densho Encyclopedia. encyclopedia.densho.org/print/Prosecution of the Shitara Sisters

Pueblo Chemical Weapons Storage Depot, www.cma.army.mil/pueblo.aspx

Pulia, Peter A., Sr. Interview by author. 1 May 2002.

Reiss, Matthias. "Bronzed Bodies behind Barbed Wire: Masculinity and the Treatment of German Prisoners of War in the United States during World War II." *The Journal of Military History* 69, No. 2 (April 2005): 475-504.

Richards, Su. Interview by author. 23 May 2009.

Rocky Mountain Arsenal, www.rma.army.mil/site/sitefrm.html

Rogers, John R. Interview by author. 3 September 2007.

Salgado, Rebecca C. "Rebuilding the Network: Interpretation of World War II Prisoner-of-War Camps in the United States." Master's Thesis, Columbia University, May 2012.

Scott, Ralph. "Violations of International Law in the Treatment of German POWs Following the Cessation of Hostilities". (Presentation, TRACES conference, 1 June 2003).

Selmi, Andrea. Interview by author. 2 November 2018.

Smith, Clarence McKittrick. *United States Army in World War II: The Technical Services: The Medical Department: Hospitalization and Evacuation, Zone of Interior.* Center of Military History, United States Army, Washington, DC, 2003.

Spidle, Jake W. Jr. "Axis Prisoners of War in the United States, 1942-1946: A Bibliographical Essay." Military Affairs 39, No. 2 (April 1975): 61-66.

"State Department-Related Sites: Hotels and Resorts," German American Internee Coalition, www.gaic.info/ShowPage.php?section=Internment_Camps

Storm, Ralph A., Camp Florence Days. N.p. 2007.

Thomas, Jennie M. "History of the Prisoner of War Camp Utah ASF Depot, Ogden, UT", 1 February 1945.

Thompson, Antonio S., *Men in German Uniform: POWs in America during World War II.* Knoxville, TN: University of Tennessee Press, 2010.

Tissing, Robert Warren Jr. "Utilization of Prisoners of War in the United States During World War II: Texas, A Case Study". Master's Thesis, Baylor University, 1973.

Todaro, Robert J. Interview by author. 12 June 2006.

Togni, Fernando. Interview by author. 14 August 2009.

Tollefson, A. M., Col., Director, Prisoner of War Operations, Letter to Special Projects Division regarding the death of Giovanni Cincotta, dated 10 January 1946, NARA RG 389, Entry 462, Box 2562. National Archives and Records Administration, College Park, MD

_____. Letter to Special Projects Division regarding the death of Giovanni E. Bondini, dated 8 June 1945, NARA RG 389, Entry 261, Box 2562. National Archives and Records Administration, College Park, MD

_____. Letter to Special Projects Division regarding Salina shooting, dated 28 August 1945, NARA RG 389, Entry 261, Box 2562. National Archives and Records Administration, College Park, MD

Trezzani, Claudio. Letter from Monticello PW Camp, AR, dated 26 January 1944. Stato Maggiore Esercito, #2256A, Rome, Italy

Turrini, Marcello. Interview by author. 22 November 2016.

Ulio, J.A., Major General, the Adjutant General's office, letter to The Commanding Generals, dated 9 April 1943. NARA RG 389, Entry 261, Box 2563. National Archives and Records Administration, College Park, MD

University of Utah. Historic Fort Douglas at the University of Utah, a Brief History & Walking Tour. Salt Lake City, UT: University of Utah, 2000.

Urwiller, Clifford S., Col. Prisoner of War Operations Division, Memorandum for Camp Operations Branch regarding surplus ISU units, dated 18 October 1945, NARA RG 389, Entry 261, Box 2563. National Archives and Records Administration, College Park, MD

_____. Memorandum for Camp Operations Branch regarding surplus ISU units, dated 14 September 1945, NARA RG 389, Entry 261, Box 2563. National Archives and Records Administration, College Park, MD

U.S. House. Report of Committee on Military Affairs. 78th Congress., 2nd sess., H. Res. 30.

U.S. House. Report of Committee on Military Affairs. 79th Congress., 1st sess., H. Res. 20.

Vecchio, Giovanni and Orazio. Interview by author. 17 November 2018.

War Department, to Commanding Generals, Regarding movement orders, dated 14 November 1945, NARA RG 389, Entry 261, Box 2563. National Archives and Records Administration, College Park, MD

_____. Regarding movement orders, dated 1 November 1945, NARA RG 389, Entry 261, Box 2563. National Archives and Records Administration, College Park, MD

_____. Regarding movement orders, dated 23 October 1945, NARA RG 389, Entry 261, Box 2563. National Archives and Records Administration, College Park, MD

_____. Regarding movement orders, dated 18 September 1945, NARA RG 389, Entry 261, Box 2563. National Archives and Records Administration, College Park, MD

Wardlow, Chester. *United States Army in World War II: The Technical Services: The Transportation Corps: Movements, Training, and Supply.* Center of Military History, United States Army, Washington, DC, 2003.

Weyand, A. M., Col. Commanding, Prisoner of War Camp, Ogden, UT, Letter regarding prisoner segregation, dated 21 January 1944, NARA RG 389, Entry 261, Box 2563. National Archives and Records Administration, College Park, MD

Whittingham, Richard. Martial Justice: the Last Mass Execution in the United States. Bluejacket Books, Naval Institute Press, Annapolis, MD. 1997

Wilcox, Walter W. "The Wartime Use of Manpower on Farms." *Journal of Farm Economics* 28, No. 3 (Aug. 1946): 723-741.

Winter, Richard. "Hot Springs, NC. A World War I Internment Camp." *North Carolina Postal Historian* 27, no. 1 (2008)

"WWI German Prisoners of War in Utah," GenTracer, www.gentracer.org/WWIGermanPrisonersofWarinUtah.html.

"WWI Internment Camp in Hot Springs, NC: The German Village," Welcome to Madison County, North Carolina, www.visitmadisoncounty.com/who-we-are/town-of-hot-springs/the-german-village-wwi-internment-camp/.

Acknowledgments

Christine Saffell (researcher and travel companion)

Kate and John Saffell (website, data entry, photos)

Alessandro de Gaetano (producer, screenwriter of Red Gold)

Andrea Boni and family (son of Guido Boni, an Italian POW)

Andrea Selmi and family (son of Carlo Selmi, an Italian POW)

Barbara Harvey (Mother, support, great memory for events in her lifetime)

Carmelina Impellizzeri (daughter of Vincenzo Lo Giudice, an Italian POW)

Carol A. Jensen (historian and author)

Dave Kendziura (historian, Hill AFB)

Gina McNeeley (photographic expert, NARA researcher)

Jinger La Guardia (colleague who shares the goal of saving these "lost" stories)

Karen Jensen and Pam Frisbie (my sisters who share the lure of the stories behind the headstones)

Karrie and Jenefer Jackson (data entry)

Kenneth D. Schlessinger (NARA II, College Park, MD)

Kent Powell (Utah Historical Society)

Marcello Turrini (son of Mario Turrini, an Italian POW)

Col. Maurizio Parri (grandson of General Dino Parri, an Italian POW)

Michael Luick-Thrams (TRACES founder)

Michael Pomeroy (authority on Camp Monticello, AR)

Orazio and Giovanni Vecchio (son/nephew and grandson of Orazio and Angelo Vecchio, Italian POW brothers)

Rhonda Jackson and Luccia Rogers (researchers)

Sarah Langsdon (Special Collections, Weber State University)

Stefano Palermo (son of Raffaele Palermo an Italian POW)

Tony Dumosch of the American Legion (authority on Greeley history)

William "Bill" Thomas of Pike's Peak Library District (authority on Camp Carson)

Please contact the author at gentracer@gmail.com to share your knowledge about prisoners of war stories, photos, letters, and artifacts that may be part of your family and local history.

Alphabetical Index